90 0360693 0

THE CHALLENGE OF
ETHNIC CONFLICT, DEMOCRACY AND
SELF-DETERMINATION
IN
CENTRAL EUROPE

The Challenge of
Ethnic Conflict, Democracy and
Self-Determination
in
Central Europe

DOV RONEN
in collaboration with and an Introduction
by
ANTON PELINKA

FRANK CASS
LONDON • PORTLAND, OR.

First Published in 1997 in Great Britain by
FRANK CASS & CO. LTD.
Newbury House, 900 Eastern Avenue
London IG2 7HH

and in the United States of America by
FRANK CASS
c/o ISBS, 5804 N.E. Hassalo Street
Portland, Oregon, 97213-3644

British Library Cataloguing in Publication Data:

A catalogue record for this book is available from the British Library

ISBN 0-7146-4752-7 (cloth)
ISBN 0-7146-4308-4 (paper)

Libary of Congress Cataloging-in-Publication Data:

A catalog record for this book is available from the Library of Congress

Typeset by Vitaset, Paddock Wood, Kent
Printed in Great Britain by
Bookcraft (Bath) Ltd, Midsomer Norton, Avon

Contents

Preface

This book is the revised version of a report on a research project conducted at the Institut für Konfliktforschung in Vienna, Austria, with funds provided by the Austrian Federal Ministry of Science and Research. Dov Ronen, the principal investigator of the research project, drafted the report submitted to the Austrian Federal Ministry as well as this revised version, save the Introduction, which appears under its author's name. It should be noted that the research was a collaborative effort. The report has been read and discussed by the other two project collaborators, Anton Pelinka and Albert Reiterer, and has been revised in light of their suggestions. Nevertheless, views presented in the Introduction rest with its author, while responsibility for the views expressed in the seven chapters rests with the principal author.

The material included here purports to provide an overall assessment of what we called 'ethnic diversity' in Central Europe, presents an hypothesis on the origins of ethnic conflict, and proposes an approach to the prevention and reduction of ethnic conflict in general and in Central Europe in particular.

Our research has not covered that entire Central Europe which, in the eyes of some, reaches from Germany in the west to Ukraine in the east. Eastern Europe was not deemed an appropriate term because present-day Austria was included in our research. East–Central–Southern Europe may have been a more accurate phrase to use, since we do include the former Yugoslavia, but it was considered awkward. Ultimately, we decided to use the label 'Central Europe'. It covers, for our purposes, roughly the geographic area of the former Austro-Hungarian and Ottoman Empires and includes Austria, Hungary, the Czech and Slovak Republics, and the countries of former

Yugoslavia: the Yugoslav Republic (including Serbia and Montenegro), Croatia, Slovenia, Bosnia-Herzegovina and Macedonia. Within those countries we do discuss most, though not all, ethnic groups.

The book is divided into two parts. Part I, The challenge of ethnic diversity, is a largely historical overview of ethnic challenges in Central Europe. It includes a case study on Yugoslavia. Part II, In search of causes and solutions, includes an analysis of the origins of conflict, propositions regarding the resolution of conflict, and concrete policy recommendations. These two parts are preceded by an introductory chapter, Ethnic conflict and democratic theory, by Anton Pelinka, and an overview titled Setting the stage.

We believe this book will be of value to students and scholars interested in conflict resolution in general and in Central Europe in particular. Beyond that, we believe that it may be useful reading to anyone willing to be challenged by what we consider to be an innovative approach to the old problems of ethnic diversity, tension and conflict.

The three collaborators on the research project were assisted by a large number of scholars at several academic institutions. Our thanks are extended to the officers and colleagues at the Institut für Konfliktforschung (Vienna, Austria), as well as at the Teleki Foundation (Budapest, Hungary), the Center for European Studies and Center for International Affairs, Harvard University (Cambridge, Massachusetts, USA), the Department of Psychiatry, Cambridge Hospital, Harvard Medical School, and the Austrian Institute for East and Southeast European Research (including its offices in Budapest, Bratislava, Brno, and Ljubljana).

We also thank the large number of individuals who have been of great help to us in various phases of this project either directly or indirectly: Viera Bacova, Felix Bister, Dano Butora, Silvo Devetak, Laszlo Dioszegi, Aleksa Djilas, Gyorgy Eger, Jasna Fischer, Sergej Flere, Valeria Heuberger, Herbai Istvan, Csaba Kiss, Matjaz Klemencic, Vladimir Klemencic, Konstantin Knitakis, Othmar Kolar, Gertrud Kothanek, Tamas Kozma, Sabine Kroissenhuber, Rudolf Kucera, Milos Kuret, Petar Lastic, Margit Mery, Alenka Mihailovski, Robert F. Miller, Albina Necak-Luk, Czibor Necas, Kalman Petocz, Richard Prazak, Andreas Pribersky, Iveta Radicova, Rudi Rizman, Davorin Senicar, Jana Starek, Arnold Supan, Stefan

Sutaj, Laszlo Szarka, Raj Tamas, Peter Tanzig, Katalin Vadkerti, Eva Varga, and Mitja Zagar.

Special thanks are also due to Mrs Reiter at the Institut für Konfliktforschung, Vienna, for her skilful administrative and logistical assistance; Saadia Touval and William Safran, both colleagues as well as friends, who read the entire manuscript and made invaluable suggestions for revisions; and to Harte Weiner for her editorial work. Responsibility for any inadvertent misinterpretation of the information and generous advice they provided is solely that of the author.

Introduction: Ethnic conflict and democratic theory

Anton Pelinka

This book reflects an academic approach to an explosive topic. The topic is the increase of ethnic tensions in the geographic region dominated by communist dictatorship for decades. Since the dismantlement of communist rule, Central Europe has become a hotbed of conflicts erupting from ethnic rivalry. For quite a time, social science has regarded ethnicity as a phenomenon in decline. Now, the increasing importance of ethnicity in Central and Eastern Europe is impossible to ignore.

The academic approach is not only to describe, analyse, and explain conflicts, but also to learn from the experiences of longer established democracies of Western Europe in their dealings with ethnic conflicts. One of the basic questions, and among the underlying interests behind this project's agenda, pertains to the way one might use democratic tools for reducing ethnic conflicts.

THE UNDERSTANDING OF DEMOCRACY

Democracy is based on a certain understanding of social conflict. The system of 'liberal democracy', as it exists today (Riker, 1982; Dahl, 1989), accepts the competition between organised interests as given fact which has to be reckoned with as an unavoidable reality. Liberal democracy sees the 'commonweal', the fictitious goal of all politics, not jeopardised by contradictions of interests and of values, but as freed by the open and therefore flexible outcome of the political process itself, which has to be accepted principally by all political actors (Fraenkel, 1964).

This openness, hence flexibility, distinguishes democracy and especially liberal democracy, from all other varieties of political systems. By contrast, the insistence that there must be a given outcome of the political process, independently from the process itself, is the beginning of totalitarian thinking. As soon as a certain political actor is completely sure that his (her) system of values and his (her) set of interests are the only right ones, and all contradicting voices are wrong and evil, the temptation begins, and those concerned conceptualise politics in an adversary mode – the forces of light against the forces of darkness.

For this very reason, democracy is antithetical to the politics of missionaries, who are bringing the true gospel to the masses of the heathens. If the permanent happiness of the masses depends on one belief only and if all competing beliefs are the route to hell, then the idea that all beliefs have to accept that the majority decides which belief is entitled to govern for a limited period of time must be anathema. Democracy is not a system to define what is 'true' – democracy is a system of entitlement to power, control of power and dismissal of the powerful. It is not truth that democracy is aiming at; it is power!

★

The changes in Europe – beginning with the tenure of Mikhail Gorbachev as Secretary-General of the Communist Party (CP) of the USSR in 1985, and leading to the dramatic collapse of communist regimes all over Europe in 1989 and 1990 – can only be compared with the tumultuous Europe between 1945 and 1948 – the years of satellisation which led to the Cold War and the balance of power between East and West during four decades. For their part, the process the former communist-ruled countries are going through has different aspects:

(1) *Democratisation*. Uniform single-party systems have broken down, making room for more or less Westernised competitive multi-party systems.
(2) *The breakthrough of market economy*. Instead of centrally planned, so-called socialist economies, we can observe the establishment of capitalist economies.

(3) *The renaissance of ethnic rivalries*. They had been suppressed for many years by a political system claiming to be completely successful in overcoming the conflicts between different ethnic groups.

We observe one other, perhaps unforeseen, result. The process of defreezing evinces itself in national antagonism, ethnic hatred and collective prejudice, all of which seem to be back from the beginning of this century – reborn and ready to take over the societies of Central and Eastern Europe – in the last years of this very century. The collapse of communist dictatorship seems to be the opening of a Pandora's box. The peoples of Central and Eastern Europe asked for democracy – and they are getting social conditions which are similar to those which existed in the Balkans in the year 1900. Have European nations also to fear new Balkan wars, resulting from those social conditions?

One might name just one indicator justifying such a fear: many sectors within the newly democratised nations in Central and Eastern Europe have lost their memory for certain painful aspects of pre-communist history. Slovak nationalists are reclaiming Josef Tiso as national hero – the same Tiso who was responsible not only for Slovakia's entry into World War II, on Germany's side, but also for dictatorship and for the implementation of the Holocaust on Slovakia's soil. Some Hungarian nationalists, on their part, seem to forget that Hungary was not a Western democracy during the inter-war period, but a semi-fascist dictatorship with anti-Jewish laws. And the Pilsudski-renaissance in present-day Poland seems to overlook the distinct anti-democratic and also anti-Semitic quality the Polish regime had before the armies of Greater Germany started their aggression against Poland. Lastly, if there is an especially tragic failure of socialist education, which the communist parties always have claimed to implement, it is the blatant lack of success in dealing with ethnic conflicts. With regard to this, the formerly communist-ruled countries in Central Europe have a lot to learn – especially from Western Europe.

CONFLICTS, INTERESTS AND CLEAVAGES

The interests democracy has to deal with emerge from the social environment. Interests have to be manifest – only manifest interests can be organised and channelled, as demands or supports, into the political system. The interests any political system has to face – and any democratic political system has to accept as, at least in principle, legitimate – are not academically constructed 'theoretical' or latent interests within society – which may be brought to life sometime in the future – but manifest interests. Manifest interests are interests which can be observed, analysed and evaluated.

Conflict emerges from clashing interests concerning the distribution of (tangible or intangible) goods. As society is characterised by scarcity, the different demands – represented by interests – cannot be fully satisfied. The consequence is conflict between different demands (and different interests). The consequence is politics.

The conflicts resulting from contradicting interests and from a given scarcity in society follow specific patterns. Marx tried to develop and describe such a pattern by using the concept of 'class'. The principal distinguishing interests, different 'classes' – defined by economic terms – were to explain the historical succession of 'basic conflicts', on which all other conflicts are based. This approach has a distinct tendency towards simplification and determinism, but provides at least some insight into the hierarchy of conflicts. The approach that Inglehart and others have broadened, developed and untied from Marx's materialistic preconditions – and which does explain the changing impact certain interests have on politics – has a triage of conflict-types. The three types of conflicts are:

(1) The 'premodern' (or 'prematerialistic') type of conflicts, which developed before industrialisation and before or at the beginning of the Enlightenment. The most important examples within this type are religious conflicts – first between different denominations, later between 'clerical' and 'secular' interests.

(2) The 'modern' (or 'materialistic') type of conflicts, resulting from the establishment of an industrialised, capitalist society. The typical conflict of this type is the conflict between 'classes', especially between labour and business (proletarians and bourgeoisie).

(3) The 'postmodern' (or 'postmaterialistic') type of conflicts, coming out from a highly industrialised society with a broad affluent and rather well educated 'middle class'. The conflicts of particular

impact, which can be subordinated under this type, are the 'gender' conflict and conflicts concerning environment.

Of course, this typology must not be seen as a strict pattern into which all conflicts have to fit. There is, for instance, the phenomenon of 'class conflict' existing even before the beginning of industrialisation. The European wars in the sixteenth century between peasants and aristocracy and the slave wars in Roman times are examples of such an overlapping reality. And the sequence of three types does not mean that the rise of new types of conflicts – for example 'postmodern' conflicts – includes the end of other, already existing, conflicts belonging to the 'older' type. Religious conflicts do reach into present times even in highly industrialised societies, as the example of Northern Ireland all too clearly indicates. These 'older' conflicts coexist with 'newer' ones, without being extinguished just by the arrival of the others. The newer types of conflict tend to rise in their importance, but without getting a kind of monopoly. And, a third reservation has to be made: there is no proof whatsoever that a reversal of the historical sequence is impossible. 'Older' conflicts, in decline for decades or centuries, can be brought back as dominating conflicts.

How do ethnic conflicts fit into this typology? Ethnic conflicts have a premodern as well as a modern aspect. They are modern, because the idea of an ethnically based 'nation-state' is the product of 'modernisation' in the sense of industrialisation and enlightenment. The 'nation-state' and the perceptions behind it are an important by-product of the European bourgeois revolutions. But ethnic conflicts have also a premodern flavour, because they appeal to non-materialistic loyalties – like religious conflicts; and because they are antithetical to the concept of 'class', at least in the Marxist sense. This is especially true of the 'pre-political' type of ethnic conflict, which, neither based nor aiming at an ethnically homogeneous 'nation-state', is premodern to a high degree. The ethnic conflicts outside Europe – India, Africa – can be seen as examples of this aspect.

The typology of conflicts can be merged with the concept of 'cleavages' (Rokkan and Urwin, 1982; Lane and Ersson, 1991). Cleavages are the phenomena which bring certain conflicts to dominate within a society. A society which is deeply fragmented by contradicting, historically rooted and well organised interests, is a society characterised by cleavages. There is no society absent of cleavages. On the other hand, their impact can vary from decisive fragmentation to 'secularised' or weary fragmentation. The concept of cleavages especially helps to explain the development of a certain party system as well as the establishment of a certain political culture.

Cleavages may also be distinguished as premodern, modern and postmodern. Like the conflict typology, this typology also does not imply a deterministic understanding of a specific historical sequence nor the necessity to completely subordinate all cleavages under one type. The typology of cleavages describes a certain trend with certain parameters – not more, but also not less.

After 1945, Western European political systems were very much under the influence of the 'materialistic' pattern. The Western European party systems followed a traditional left-right scale, and electoral behaviour was strongly determined by the class factor. At the same time, a network of corporatist power-sharing between business and labour was helpful in stabilising Western European political systems; but, again, by underlining the materialist character. Yet, compromise between class interests produced, and was defined as, stability. Those interests considered 'pre-materialist' or 'non-materialist' were 'secondary', and were dealt with in a rather successful way. Examples are the solutions of many cases of ethnic conflict by guaranteeing autonomy for minorities: as in Italy for the French-speaking minority in the Aosta valley, and as for the German-speaking minority in South Tyrol; as in Germany for the Danish-speaking minority in Schleswig-Holstein; as in Switzerland by the power balance among the three main linguistic groups (already established in the nineteenth century and rejuvenated by the solution of the delicate Jura-problem in the early 1970s); as in Spain after the end of the Franco-regime, in the cases of Basque and Catalan autonomy.

Thus, the set of rules used for the successful solution of ethnic conflicts in Western Europe after 1945 originates in the idea of power sharing. All ethnic interests, strong enough for creating fragmentations, were invited to participate within the power structure of the political system. According to the model of 'consociational democracy' which Lijphart deduced from the realities of European politics, the solution of ethnic conflicts – solution not in the sense of an end of those conflicts, but in the sense of stabilising the political system despite ethnic fragmentation – is either 'separation' within a federal system (as in the case of the French-speaking part of the canton Berne, which became the new canton Jura), or, ethnic power sharing on a sub-federal level (as in the case of South Tyrol). The second variation is successful only if the ethnic group, considered to be 'minority' on the national level (like the German-speaking population in South Tyrol), is enabled to play the role of 'majority' on the sub-federal level, that is, within the autonomous province of South Tyrol (Bolzano).

FRAGMENTATION AND DEMOCRACY

The depth of cleavages in a specific society is a factor with particular impact on democracy. Even though democracy needs consensus, a specific cleavage must not prevent a minimum of common under-standing that democracy needs. This consensus the democratic procedure is built upon has two levels:

(1) *The level concerning political substance.* It pertains to the consensus on basic human rights that each individual is entitled to without regard to class or religion, gender, ethnicity or 'race'. This consensus consists especially of the guarantee of no interference with these rights.
(2) *The level concerning political procedure.* This is the consensus regarding respect for the political process and its result. The rules of the electoral and any other decision-making process must be accepted – by winners and losers.

The consensus on both levels is a kind of 'prevention of politics'. The consensus itself is not part of the competition; different interests are legitimate in a democracy. But a deeply fragmented society tends to politicise the consensus on both levels. A deeply frag-mented society tends to transform politics into the fight between 'good' and 'evil'; and with 'evil', consensus is neither thinkable nor possible.

Empirical evidence for the destructive force of deep fragmentation includes the civil wars of the nineteenth and twentieth centuries. The breakdown of a minimum-consensus – independently from the question of responsibility – is the final reason for civil wars: in the United States 1861, in Austria 1934, in Spain 1936, in (post-) Yugoslavia 1991; and also in Pakistan 1971, in Liberia 1990 and in Rwanda 1994. If the consensus cannot stay alive, as the consequence of fragmentation is too deeply rooted, democracy is endangered.

But there is also empirical evidence that democracy is able to adapt and to develop specific rules to deal with deep fragmentation. According to Lehmbruch (Lehmbruch, 1967), this ability to adapt is more or less bound to the traumatic experience of the collapse of consensus. It is only after such a trauma that the necessity, not only to rebuild consensus but to strengthen it by new means, is broadly accepted. The lesson – cases like Switzerland, the Netherlands, Austria and Spain, but also Colombia and, with lesser success and only for brief periods, Lebanon and Cyprus – is the partial retreat of competitive democracy in favour of consociational democracy (Lijphart, 1977).

Because competition is a constitutive part of any democracy, consociational democracy does not mean the end of open competition between different and contradicting interests, but rather the strengthening of the procedural part of consensus making. And in consociational democracy the principal rule, which has to be added to the usual set of rules in any democracy, is the rule of power sharing: any interest important (and strong) enough to jeopardise the consensus has to be invited to participate in the power structure, at the top of the political hierarchy.

This general rule of reducing democratic competition and of power sharing can be implemented in different ways:

• **Grand coalition.** This is especially the pattern Switzerland has established as a consequence of the fragmentation between Catholics and Protestants, but also between German and non-German (mainly French-) speaking Swiss. The Swiss grand coalition has been composed for decades of the four biggest parties in parliament, which represent the major elements of Swiss society, and balancing (linguistic or ethnic) German interests (usually represented by four out of seven members of the Federal Council, that is, the cabinet) and non-German interests. They include the Protestants (mainly represented by the Free Democrats (FDP) and the Swiss People's Party (SVP)), Catholics (mainly represented by the Christian Democratic People's Party (CVP)), and 'secular' interests (mainly represented by the Social Democrats (SPS), as well as the right (the bourgeois parties) and left (SPS)).

• **Autonomy**. This model has been developed in the cases of Finland (concerning the Aaland islands, populated by a majority of Swedish-speaking Finnish citizens); Italy (for South Tyrol as well as for the French-speaking Aosta valley); Spain (for Catalonia and the Basque country) and others. The leading philosophy is to give a group (especially a group defined as an ethnic entity) – which is a minority on the national level but geographically concentrated in a specific area – majority status in a given regional unit. This results in a high degree of political autonomy. The (national) majority – (ethnic) Finns, Italians, Spaniards – is to be transformed into an ethnic minority on this particular regional level.

• **Corporatism**. This pattern tries to overcome fragmentation by 'class' cleavage through a network of participation and co-determination, binding business and labour to a political procedure, which makes consensus a precondition for decisions. Corporatism, as established in post-1945 Austria (but also in Scandinavian countries, in the Netherlands and – to a lesser degree – in Germany) is a recipe for power sharing between class interests, by integrating 'basic' interest groups (labour unions, employers' associations) into decision-making bodies within the 'black box' of the political system, and guaranteeing both sides (labour and business) veto power in all main issues (Lehmbruch and Schmitter, 1982).

• **Consociationalism within one dominating party**. The case of India demonstrates that despite open democratic competition, one party (the Congress Party) can integrate the main conflicting social (caste), ethnic (language group), and religious interests into its own party structure and dominate the still competitive party system by an in-built consensus. Because this particular party is cross-cutting through all major interests (Hindus and Muslims and Sikhs, upper and lower castes, main linguistic groups from the north as well as from the south), it has been able to play the role of a hegemon confronted with parties which speak for special interests and much less for all of them.

Consociational democracy, as power sharing and as a mechanism for reducing democratic competition, is of special importance for 'cleavages', dividing interests unavoidably defined as 'majority' and 'minority'. If a minority by definition does not have the chance to become majority – most poignantly as in the instance of Northern Ireland's Catholics, or the Muslims in India as examples for religious fragmentation, and plainly in instances of ethnic fragmentation (Tutsis in Rwanda and Burundi, Hungarians in Romania, or Roma in Hungary, Romania or Slovakia, Turks in Bulgaria or Russians in the Baltic States, Quebecois in Canada or Chinese in Malaysia, 'Whites' in South Africa or 'Blacks' in the United States) – the simple application of majority rule without principal amendments is the guarantee of destabilisation, violence and human rights violations. Their results, in turn, are either the open dictatorship of a minority-based government (for example, South Africa's apartheid) or the exclusion of the (ethnically, not politically defined) minority from any participation in government (as was the case in the United States before the civil rights and voting rights legislation in the 1960s).

The exclusion of any significant, ethnically defined group from political participation – whether legally based or *de facto* exclusion – undermines the legitimacy of the political system. It need not even be an exclusion, as the example of Bosnia-Herzegovina demonstrates: The simple refusal of the Bosnian Serbs to accept Bosnia-Herzegovina's independence destroyed the stability of this state, designed to be a sovereign as well as a democratic system, from its very beginning. To have a democratic and stable political system, all significant interests have to accept the system itself and its basic rules. The invitation to participate in a pattern of power sharing is helpful but cannot guarantee democratic stabilisation. Without such an invitation, stabilisation in an ethnically fragmented society does not seem possible.

CROSS-CUTTING CLEAVAGES AND DEMOCRATIC STABILIZATION

As Lijphart (Lijphart, 1977) has demonstrated in the case of Switzerland, cross-cutting through different cleavages improves the chance of stabilisation by consociationalism. In Switzerland, the linguistic cleavage (German versus French) and the religious cleavage (Protestants versus Catholics) are not at all parallel. On the contrary: both the French- and the German-speaking cantons are more or less evenly divided between regions of Catholic and Protestant hegemony. On the other level, it means that Catholic cantons are also evenly divided between the two major linguistic groups as are the Protestant cantons.

This means moderation: any religious conflict is cross-cutting through linguistic loyalties, and any linguistic (ethnic) conflict does the same with respect to religious loyalties. If in a particular case this moderation through cross-cutting does not work – as when the French-speaking and Catholic north-western part of the canton Berne was opposed principally against the domination by the Protestant and German-speaking majority – the solution was secession. The new canton, Jura, was created by separating the French-speaking Catholic region from the main part of Berne.

In Switzerland, the possibility of peaceful separation is built upon a political culture of consensus orientation, power sharing and the regular awareness of the cross-cutting character. These are the main cleavages Switzerland is characterised by. The comparison with the post-Yugoslav collapse gives a significant picture: because, in the case of Yugoslavia, ethnic and religious cleavages overlap, any moderation of cross-cutting could not take place. And because the ethnic identity of Serbs, Croats and Muslims was the same as the religious identity of Orthodox, Catholics and Muslims, since ethnicity, at least in the case of Muslims, has been (and still is) the direct consequence of religious affiliation, the two cleavages (religious and ethnic) are multiplying fragmentation.

In Central and Eastern Europe we have many cases of parallel ethnic and religious cleavages: it is the case in Bulgaria (Bulgarians/Orthodox versus Turks/Muslims), in Lithuania (Lithuanians/Catholics versus Russians/Orthodox), and in Azerbaidjan (Azeris/Muslims versus

Armenians/Orthodox). The comparative ease with which Czechs and Slovaks were able to sustain their separation can be seen as the result of the absence of a second cleavage, in addition to the existing ethnic (national) one.

Western Europe's ethnic conflicts are not always the story of undisputed successes: Belgium – despite the improvements the new constitution was able to deliver – is still deeply fragmented in a rather hostile way according to linguistic differences. Northern Ireland is its most dramatic failure: in this case, Western European democracy was not able at all to find a model of conflict solution for one of the most explosive cases of pre-materialist cleavages: a conflict between Protestants and Catholics. Nevertheless, compared with its past, Western Europe entered the 1990s with a rather successful record in dealing with pre-materialist as well as materialist cleavages; Western Europe has concentrated more and more on the cleavages so typical for this highly industrialised continent. They include:

- The environment, which is becoming more and more one of the most mobilising political topics, even responsible for the creation of a new 'party family' in Europe – the Greens.
- The gender factor, which is responsible for one of the most significant general factors of European politics in the 1980s – the constant rise of female power in politics.
- The generation factor, expressed in the correlation of age and voting and influenced by the different chances the society was able to prepare for different generations.

PATTERNS OF ETHNIC CONFLICT

Ethnic conflicts in Central and Eastern Europe are to be seen according to the following patterns: international ethnic conflicts and intranational ethnic conflicts.

International ethnic conflicts are conflicts cross-cutting existing international borders. Ethnic fragmentation in those cases includes the possibility of conflicts between sovereign states as well as the possibility of policies aimed at the (more or less peaceful) redrawing of boundaries between sovereign states. The usual pattern of international ethnic conflicts is that one state claims the role of advocate for an ethnic group within the borders of another state.

There are many examples of such conflicts in Central and Eastern Europe. They include the already articulated conflict between Hungary and Romania concerning the Hungarian minority in Transylvania; the possible conflict, not yet articulated openly, between Hungary and Slovakia concerning the Hungarian minority in Slovakia; the conflict between Turkey and Bulgaria about the Turkish minority in southern Bulgaria, which was already activated during the last years of the communist regime in Bulgaria; the long-standing conflict between Bulgaria and (former) Yugoslavia concerning Macedonia and the Macedonians, that is, a people, who are, according to official Bulgarian attitude, part of the Bulgarian people; the conflict between Albania and Serbia about the Albanian population, the ethnic majority in the autonomous Serbian province of Kosovo; the conflict between Romania and the Ukraine about the Moldavians, a people Romania considers to be Romanian and who form an ethnic majority within the Soviet republic of Moldavia; the conflict between Poland and the former Soviet republics, concerning the Polish minority in some border regions, especially in Lithuania. This conflict is of explosive importance considering the establishment of Lithuanian independence and therefore linking an international to an intranational ethnic conflict.

Intranational ethnic conflicts are conflicts between ethnic groups within existing internationally recognised borders – thus without the international legal right of interference by another sovereign state, which might be claiming the role of ethnic advocate. Intranational ethnic conflicts can jeopardise the existence of a sovereign state, threatening the break-up of such a state into two or more new states. The collapse of the Austro-Hungarian 'Dual Monarchy' in 1918 is such an example.

The cases of such intranational conflict in Eastern Europe are numerous – to say the least. The mere existence of two multiethnic federations, the USSR and Yugoslavia, so significant for the European order established after 1945, had been based on the assumed capacity to surmount intranational ethnic conflicts within the federation. Both were based on the constitutional compromise between an ethnic group (or nation) with some traditions of claiming a leading role: the

Russians in the case of the USSR, the Serbs in the case of Yugoslavia. Another country, which had also been strongly affected by intranational ethnic conflicts, the Czecho-Slovak Federal Republic, was also based on a compromise between Czechs and Slovaks. The possible explosion of ethnic conflict within currently respected international borders is perhaps especially great in those political units, which had been successfully claiming full independence from the central institutions in Moscow or Belgrade. For instance, between the Serbian minority living in Croatia and the Croatian majority; or between the Russian minority and the Estonian majority in Estonia; or between the Ossetians, an ethnic group in the Caucasus, and the Georgian majority in Georgia.

As these cases of intranational ethnic conflict clearly demonstrate, there is no simple solution to ethnic conflicts in Central and Eastern Europe. There can be no solution by simply redrawing borders or by guaranteeing independence to certain regions. There is no simple solution because there are no clear ethnic frontiers in Central and Eastern Europe. All over the region there is the dominating phenomenon of 'ethnic pockets' within 'ethnic pockets'. For instance, the Latvians in the former USSR could have been called an ethnic minority, confronted by the majority of ethnic Russians. But in Latvia the Russians are an ethnic minority, confronted by the Latvians, who are not even a clear majority, but just a plurality among different ethnic groups – Russians, Lithuanians and Estonians, Ukrainians, Byelo-Russians, Germans, and Jews who, according to the former legal Soviet doctrine, are considered to be an ethnic group. And there is no region within Latvia populated only by Russians. Russians are spread all over Latvia. In some parts of Latvia, such as in Riga, Russians used to be the largest ethnic group. To accord Latvia full independence may have been a good idea – may also be legitimate due to democratic principles, justified as a kind of historical justice, considering the fate of Latvia in 1940 – but Latvia's independence did not solve the existing ethnic conflicts. Independence only meant the transferring of those conflicts from the level of a huge federation to the level of a comparatively small state.

The already mentioned case of ethnic conflicts between Georgians and Ossetians in the Soviet Republic of Georgia demonstrates another aspect of possible explosion: on 31 March 1991, an overwhelming majority of voters in Georgia backed the policy of Georgia's government to seek full independence from Moscow. At the very same time, the Georgian parliament in Tbilisi cancelled the autonomy the region of South Ossetia had enjoyed within the constitution of the USSR. Georgian nationalism, understandably claiming the values of democracy and self-determination in justifying its bid for independence, was not willing to permit a lower degree of self-rule within Georgia for a non-Georgian minority living in a specific area. And there is the similar case of Serbian nationalism: in spring 1991, the ruling party in Serbia, backed by a large majority of votes, came out in favour of the annexation of a small region in Croatia, inhabited by a majority of Serbs. But the very same Serbian nationalism is responsible for abolishing the autonomy which the province of Kosovo enjoyed within the Republic of Serbia for many years, under the auspices of the constitution of 1972. In both cases, nationalism had been claiming democratic values for challenging the communist order – but the same nationalism was not willing to tolerate certain rights of other ethnic groups.

Ethnic conflicts in Eastern Europe are even more explosive because there are in most cases no cross-cutting religious factors akin to those that exist in Switzerland to soften ethnic tensions. Almost all Serbs are Orthodox Christians – there is no significant Catholic minority among Serbs. Croats are overwhelmingly Catholics – there is no significant Orthodox minority among Croats. Hungarians in Romania are either Protestant or Catholic – but they are not Orthodox like almost all ethnic Romanians. The fragmentation between Turks and ethnic Bulgarians in Bulgaria is hardened by the fact that this fragmentation is also the fragmentation between Muslims and Christians. The civil-war-like situation between Azeris and Armenians in Azerbaidjan is hardened because Azeris are traditionally homogeneous Muslims, and Armenians are in the same way Christians. Ethnicity and religion in Eastern Europe are usually parallel factors – religion playing a decisive role in creating ethnic identity.

This situation is responsible for the cleavages surfacing after the collapse of communist regimes. There is no indication that the above mentioned postmaterialist factor will be dominating political parties and party competition in Eastern Europe: and there is not even an indication that it will be the materialist factor which will create political structures in Eastern Europe. It is not the class cleavage which characterises the political landscape of Central and Eastern Europe today; that is, for example, the reason why – against all predictions – social democratic parties did very poorly during the first elections in Poland, Hungary, CSFR, Croatia and Slovenia. It is the ethnic cleavage and, to a certain extent, the religious cleavage, which most characteristically explain the outcome of those first elections under the auspices of a multi-party system. While Western Europe is more and more dominated by post-materialism, Central and Eastern European democracies started with a rebirth of pre-materialism.

It is like in a game, the players have to go back to square one. After the paralysis of communist regimes, Central and Eastern European societies are discovering Western style democracy. They are beginning to enjoy the absence of political oppression, the absence of a power monopoly. But instead of reshaping their political systems according to the experiences of Western European states in the post-World War II era, Central and Eastern European countries seem to fall back into a Europe of the beginning of our century. It has been a Europe very much characterised by nationalism, by ethnic tensions, by wars, justified by nationalistic interests. It has been typified by the lack of ethnic and religious tolerance. The new democracies in Central and Eastern Europe seem to be very much influenced by the Europe of the Balkan wars and of the traditional German-French rivalries – and much less by a Europe which Adenauer, De Gaulle, DeGasperi and Churchill have tried to establish. Central and Eastern Europe have not only to rediscover democracy, but also history. They have to discover the simple fact that there is no standstill in social development, that European peace and European democracy are European experiences to be learned. For Europe to be a continent of peace and democracy, history must go forward – not backward.

REFERENCES

R.A. Dahl, *Democracy and its Critics* (Yale University Press, 1989).
E. Fraenkel, *Deutschland und die westlichen Demokratien* (Stuttgart, 1964).
J.-E. Lane and S.O. Ersson, *Politics and Society in Western Europe* (Sage, 1991).
G. Lehmbruch, *Proporzdemokratie: Politisches System und Politische Kultur in der Schweiz und in Osterreich* (Tubingen, 1967).

G. Lehmbruch and P.C. Schmitter, *Patterns of Corporatist Policy Making* (Sage, 1982).
A. Lijphart, *Democracy in Plural Societies: A Comparative Exploration* (New Haven, 1977).
W.H. Riker, *Liberalism against Populism* (Freeman, 1982).
S. Rokkan and D. Urwin, eds, *The Politics of Territorial Identity: Studies in European Regionalism* (Sage, 1982).

Setting the stage

The collapse of the Berlin Wall in November 1989 marked the end of the Cold War with greater clarity than any recent event. The instantly televised mingling of East and West Berliners rightly stood as a symbol for the end of a decades-old division of the world into two rival camps. The end of the Cold War also held the promise of dramatic and meaningful changes. While during the Cold War processes of democratisation and economic reforms could proceed only on the western side of the Iron Curtain, the end of the Cold War opened the door to democratisation and economic reform in the new states emerging from the formerly communist-ruled world as well. Vistas of the coming peaceful World Order contained sprawling networks of political and economic relations among governments and among peoples of democratic states around the world.

It did not take long for the eruption of extreme nationalist manifestations and ethnic conflict to threaten, and in some instances actually disrupt, the newly initiated processes of democratisation and economic reform. Within a short two years of the collapse of the Berlin Wall, prospects for the expected smooth transition to a peaceful new World Order also waned. The unexpected end of the Cold War at the time it occurred was followed by a similarly unexpected eruption of ethnic conflicts at the time and place they did.

The early 1990s ethnic conflicts, by which we refer here to conflicts between groups and between a group and the government primarily on the basis of language and or religion, were not unprecedented. They erupted earlier and in various regions. They had come in waves and leaped from one part of the world to another, from one type of social, political and economic condition to other types. For example, many of the post World War II ethnic awakenings in the late 1960s and early 1970s erupted in the industrialised countries of Western Europe: among Basques and Catalan in Spain, Scots and Welsh in Great Britain, Flemings and Walloons in Belgium, Alsatians, Bretons and Corsicans in France, and German-speakers in the Jura of Switzerland.[1] There were others, in the same period, in other parts of the world, such as in Canada, Nigeria and India. But, by the late 1970s the intensity of those conflicts diminished and, although it never truly disappeared, 'ethnicity' did not seem to be a major issue for years for either scholars or policy makers.

Ethnicity and the 'nationality problem' in the communist world drew only marginal scholarly, political and public interest in the West during the entire length of the Cold War years. They were rarely focused on. Most area and country specialists discussed these issues in wider contexts. Thus the 'nationality problem' in Yugoslavia was followed closely by specialists focusing on Yugoslavia in the context of Tito's rule; western Soviet specialists on the other hand were primarily concerned, even as late as the mid-1980s, with the intensifying policies of linguistic and cultural 'Russification' in the non-Russian Republics of the Soviet Union rather than with ethnicity *per se*.

Lack of specific interest in these aspects of political life in the communist world was probably not accidental. During the Cold War years there appeared to be a clear-cut dichotomy between democracy and totalitarianism, freedom and repression, private enterprise and state control, defence of the free world versus military expansionism – and nationalism versus internationalism. 'Ethnicity' did not become a useful concept within the rigid parameters of Cold War rhetoric.

Even the rise of Gorbachev to power in 1985, the introduction of *glasnost* and *perestroika* in the Soviet Union and freedom for former satellites of the Soviet Union, barely raised the spectre of ethnic discontent. Gorbachev's reforms implied a gradual process of decentralisation, that is, giving greater power to governments of the Soviet republics. In the former satellite countries of the Soviet Union a process of democratisation was launched. Mikhail Gorbachev received the Nobel Peace Prize, in the view of most onlookers rightly so, presumably because of the belief that the reforms he introduced would propel change toward pluralistic democracy and stability in the formerly communist world and toward a more peaceful world overall. Cheering Western onlookers had not yet become aware of the 'ethnic question' behind the fallen Iron Curtain in the first years of Gorbachev's presidency. The main public concern in the Western world at the time was not ethnic conflict, but whether NATO alone, or the demonstration effect of democracy, the private enterprise system, effectiveness of Western radio and television broadcasts, and/or the Star Wars project of President Reagan too, should be credited with the victory of democracy in Eastern Europe.

Ethnicity, and extreme nationalism in their variations, were still insignificant terms even as late as 1991. True enough, the Lithuanian parliament had declared independence already in March 1990 and the parliaments of the other two Baltic states, Latvia and Estonia, in August 1991. Also, the virtual disfranchisement of Russian inhabitants in Estonia that preceded this declaration may be seen as a 'nationalist' manifestation. However, the declarations of independence by their respective parliaments and the subsequent secessions of all three Baltic states was regarded in the Western world as no more than the rightful restoration of independent *statehood* lost in 1940.

Arguably, even the secession of other Union republics from the Soviet Union was regarded as the *relegitimation* of their sovereign existence, rather than resurgent nationalism. True enough, the separation from Russia could easily be seen as assertion of national identities. However, at the time the Soviet Union broke up, as late as 1991, nationalism and ethnic conflict were still relegated to a category of temporary side-effects of the transition to democracy.

Ethnic conflict, as a problem, was given prominence only as the first conflicts erupted between Croats and Slovenes on the border area between the two autonomous republics of Yugoslavia, and between Serbs and Croats in Croatia. The violent ethnic conflict in Bosnia, and the resurgence of nationalist manifestations in other parts of Eastern and Central Europe, provided the final push. It was the conflict in Bosnia-Herzegovina which revived public interest, and propelled scholarly concern with ethnic conflict.

The eruption of ethnic conflicts and the resurgence of extreme nationalism in the formerly communist world also posed a challenge to foreign policy makers.

Western policies traditionally sided with national aspirations, the right to self-determination and the territorial integrity of states. The break-up of the Soviet Union did not require a policy change since not merely a state but the Soviet *communist empire*, and the Cold War rival, was breaking up. Thus, it was relatively easy, to use an example, to justify Ukrainian nationalism, recognise the Ukrainians' right to self-determination, and support the territorial integrity of the newly independent Ukraine. However, the pending breaking up of Yugoslavia, not a Soviet satellite since 1948, did not present such a clear-cut case. It was not at all clear if '*Bosnian-Herzegovians*' have a right to self-determination and whether to vouch for the territorial integrity of Bosnia-Herzegovina – or Yugoslavia. Western foreign policies vacillated on *these* issues.

There may be another relevant point. While a smooth transition to democracy after the end of the Cold War was expected to allow a relaxation of Western military preparedness, the eruption of ethnic conflicts dictated a wait-and-see policy. Beyond that, and maybe most importantly, it was not at all clear to policy makers who was friend and who the foe, and which side should receive international political and possible military support. In the emerging chaotic situation it was difficult to pinpoint an obvious enemy!

Ultimately, members of the then European Community and the United States, the most important international players, did take a stand. They acknowledged the right to self-determination of the breakaway states of Slovenia and Croatia, recognised their independent status and held applicable to them the principle of territorial integrity. However, the eruption of violent conflicts, especially between Serbs and Muslims in Bosnia-Herzegovina in the immediate aftermath of United States recognition, did not put the troubling issues to rest. While the right of self-determination was transferred to Bosnia-Herzegovina and its territorial integrity was to be safeguarded, the national aspirations of the Bosnian Serbs – and Bosnian Croats – could not be dismissed unequivocally. Why?

It is undeniable that Bosnia-Herzegovina, being one of the six republics of former Yugoslavia, had more evident right to independent status than Bosnian Serbs. But there were additional aspects to consider which were probably among the ones that delayed the decision of recognition. First, the population of Bosnia-Herzegovina was far more heterogeneous than those of either Slovenia or Croatia, and no ethnic group had a clear numerical majority. Second, Bosnian-Serbs did not so much ask for independence as for a form of autonomy or cantonal status which did indeed become the topic for later negotiations. Third, at least the Wilsonian principle of self-determination refers to the rights of 'people', which the Serbs, as a whole, may be considered to be. That autonomous Bosnian-Serbs would have joined Serbia was a separate, political, issue which had little if anything to do with the applicability of the principle itself.

The dilemma that the Bosnian Serb aspiration posed to foreign policy makers and to concerned public opinion was 'solved' by the introduction of the phrase 'ethnic cleansing' into the political vocabulary. While the phrase 'ethnic conflict' merely conveyed a conflictual relationship between two or more groups and did not readily convey an aggressor–victim relationship, 'ethnic cleansing' did. 'Ethnic cleansing', used as a label for such atrocities as raping, burning, and expelling of innocent civilians, did convey an aggressor–victim relationship and appeared as a clearly objectionable act which foreign policy makers could easily target.

Furthermore, 'ethnic cleansing' could be seen as not only *morally* abhorrent but also as *politically* unacceptable. The act of 'ethnic cleansing', quite apart from implying the sowing of death and destruction, also appeared to contradict a widely held Western approach to ethnic diversity. The widely subscribed to scholarly and policy approach has long held national integration, nation-building, democratic pluralism as guiding principles for ethnically heterogeneous countries in general and in the ethnically diverse countries of the 'Third World' in particular. Although actual implementation has at times deviated from the principle, perhaps Switzerland is one such example, the creation of ethnically homogeneous states has not been accepted in principle. Consequently, those who engage in 'ethnic cleansing' are not only seen to be engaged in criminal acts and even genocide, they are also perceived as proponents of politically unacceptable practices akin to apartheid, segregation and racism.

The argument we are submitting here begins with the proposition that 'ethnicity' in general and 'ethnic conflict' in particular are complex phenomena, and in the area covered by the former Yugoslavia they appeared in all their complexity. There was the confusing pattern of traditional hostilities during the long-lasting Ottoman rule, the shifting alliances and bloody confrontations during two Balkan wars, the rivalries and fragile alliances before and after World

War I, the atrocities by Nazi allied elements against Serbs, Jews and Gypsies during World War II, and the not too clearly understood ethnic relations during Tito's rule. The introduction of the phrase 'ethnic cleansing', we argue, was readily welcomed by observers, for it clarified the complex picture and simplified it. It helped to pinpoint Serbs as the aggressors, thus the potential enemy in political and military context, and the 'cleansed' Muslims as the victims, hence the potential friends and allies. The successful substitution of the phrase 'ethnic cleansing' for 'ethnic conflict' provided foreign policy makers and public opinion not only with a moral but also an ideological, hence political, reference point. Scholars and decision makers who had difficulty locating Croatia on the map and had, at best, cursory knowledge of the history and culture of the various peoples in the region, could now express an informed opinion.[2]

By the second half of 1995, the phrase 'ethnic cleansing' has largely faded from the vocabulary, as acts labelled by this term have waned. Elsewhere in Central Europe, the separation between Czechs and Slovaks was peaceful, negotiations about Hungarian minorities in Slovakia and in Romania are ongoing, and in Bosnia-Herzegovina a federal arrangement was agreed to between Bosnian Croats and Muslims. Overall, the threat that nationalist manifestations and ethnic conflicts posed just a few years ago seem to have subsided considerably in Central Europe.

Nevertheless, it would be foolish to assume that the re-emergence or intensification of ethnic conflict is no longer possible. As the recent eruption of conflicts was a surprise to most, so future eruptions will likely be, unless a better understanding of its possible causes is reached, and ways of reducing, preventing, and ending ethnic conflict is better understood. These are the ambitious aims of this book.

NOTES

1. Walker Connor, 'Ethnonationalism in the First World: The Present in Histori-
    cal Perspective', in Milton J. Esman, ed., *Ethnic Conflict in the Western World*
    (Ithaca: Cornell University Press, 1977), pp. 20– 21.
2. It may be of interest to know that the phrase 'ethnic cleansing', which helped to
    shape public opinion and aim foreign policies against a polarised enemy, has
    entered the public and diplomatic vocabulary quite accidentally. We shall
    describe this event in some detail in Chapter 5.

Part I
The challenge of ethnic diversity

1 The ethnic mosaic in Central Europe

Central Europe is an ethnic mosaic, a region of great ethnic diversity. Part I is devoted to an overview of the challenge that ethnic diversity has posed over the years and this first chapter provides a sketchy overview of the degree and scope of ethnic diversity in Central Europe and highlights specific events which may have been particularly relevant to the formation of that diversity.

This chapter is not intended to be analytical in any meaningful sense of the word. Instead, it includes a rather dry encyclopaedic summary of information from secondary sources and provides succinct descriptions of the various groups' histories. There was an attempt to account for most, though not all, groups. On the other hand, we did not even attempt to provide all relevant historical data. The main purpose of this chapter is to assist the non-specialist in grasping the scope of diversity in the region and the historical background to post-Cold War ethnic conflicts. The specialist, in turn, will be able to assess our judgement as to what to include and to exclude. This chapter is also intended to provide background material for our subsequent assessment of ongoing and potential conflicts among various groups, all of which are rooted in that diversity.

A BRIEF HISTORICAL OVERVIEW TO 1918

Most of the inhabitants of Central Europe are latter-day descendants of migrants coming from both East and West, some as early as the sixth and seventh centuries. Some of the early migrant groups settled alongside other groups for a while, then migrated elsewhere. Other migrating groups settled in a specific location and stayed. Peaceful

4 The challenge of ethnic conflict

relations over the centuries were intermittent with bloody conflicts among the various groups.

What seems to us significant is that, in the area we are concentrating on, there are three predominant *language families*: Slav, German, and Hungarian (Magyar).[1] Albanians and, arguably, many Macedonians, do not 'belong' to any of these language families. Nor does the tripartite linguistic division imply homogeneity within each language group. Czech and Serbian, for example, are two different languages. Furthermore, members of each of the three groups may, at times, find distinctions within the group greater than across groups, on one or another basis. Thus some Czechs, members of the Slav linguistic family, at times have found greater affinity to some members of the German or Hungarian linguistic families than to, say, Serb members of the Slav linguistic family.

The tripartite classification does indicate, however, that, due to early migrations, Central Europe had become the meeting place of three linguistic families whose heritage and early cultural patterns differed from each other. Thus we shall see, for example, that descendants of the eighteenth-century German settlers in Croatia on the Hungarian border were still considered Germans in the twentieth century, at least in part because of differences in heritage and early cultural patterns.

In addition to language families there are in Central Europe three major religions: Western Christianity, Eastern Christianity, and Islam. Again, this tripartite division does not imply that only members of these three religions inhabit Central Europe. There are other religions that do not belong to any of these three main religions. Nor does it mean homogeneity within each group. Members of each of the three religions may, at times, find distinctions within each religion greater than across religions. But the presence of the three religions does indicate significant diversity; Central Europe had become a meeting place of world religions, each with its international ties and implications.[2]

An additional comment should be made about political units in Central Europe. In the distant past migratory groups settled *in regions*, such as 'next to today's Switzerland', or 'in the Carpathian mountains'. The resulting ethnic mosaic was formed within those regions, or geographic areas, which had no delineated political boundaries.

Some of these migrant groups are said to form 'states' or 'empires'. It must be noted, however, that not all such 'empires' and 'states' were organised political entities. Often conquered *regions* were designated as the 'Empire of ...' or the 'Kingdom of ...', named after a conqueror or a dominant group of people. For example, in an historical atlas one may find the 'Empire of Attila' (the Hun) at around AD 450. This empire did range from beyond the Volga river in the east to today's Holland in the west, and from today's Sweden in the north to somewhere around today's Switzerland and Greece in the south. But, there was no political unity to the 'Empire of Attila' in the modern sense of the word. It consisted of a multitude of subdued groups, 'tribes', some paying tribute to the Hun ruler, while others, for lengthy periods, did not. Thus, ethnic diversity in such 'states' or 'empires' had far different implications than the same in territorially delineated states and empires of more recent times.

We shall turn now to a brief narrative on each of the three linguistic groups. Within each section we shall proceed chronologically, first focusing on early migrations and proceeding to the present.

THE SLAVIC-SPEAKING PEOPLES

It is said that the Slavs[3] of Central Europe probably originated in the region of Galicia (north-east of today's Hungary). Driven in the sixth century by the Avars, they migrated southward and westward, reaching as far as the central part of today's Germany. From that period on, roughly the seventh century, the Slavic peoples were regarded as divided into three main language groups:

1. **West Slavs**: Poles, Czechs, Slovaks, Lusatians and other smaller groups of which several still exist today.
2. **South Slavs**: Serbs, Croats, Slovenes, many (or most) Macedonians, Montenegrins, Bosnians, Bulgars (not the proto-Bulgarians of the sixth to eighth centuries who were not Slav in origin).
3. **East Slavs**: Great Russians, Ukrainians, Byelorussians (White Russians).

We shall now provide a brief commentary, among West Slavs, on:

Czechs, Slovaks and Lusatians; and, among South Slavs on: Serbs, Croats, Slovenes, Macedonians, Montenegrins and Bosnians. At the end of each commentary section, a few among the most salient features of the group will be summarised under the heading: '**Distinct features that may be factors in a conflict**'. As the heading implies, a listed feature – such as religion, language, historical memory – distinguishes a group from its neighbours and may be one of the factors in past, present and possibly future conflict.

Southern Slavs

The Serbs, probably _some_ Serbs, migrated to the Balkans in the sixth and seventh centuries and converted to Orthodox Christianity in the ninth century, when the first Serb political formation emerged in the Bosnian mountains under the name of Rascia. In 1159 Stephen Nemanja established a royal dynasty and received the blessings of the Byzantine Emperor. His son, in turn, received the blessings of the Pope in Rome in 1217 – as king. However, his brother, Sava, then the archbishop of Belgrade, appealed to and received in 1219 the recognition of the patriarch of Constantinople for an autocephalous Serbian Orthodox Church. By the mid-fourteenth century there emerged a large entity called the Kingdom of Servia under one Stephan Dushan, who became king in 1331 and tsar in 1346. It was in 1389 that the Ottoman Turks – coming from the Anatolian mountains in today's Turkey – defeated the Serbs in the famous Battle of Kosovo. It is this battle which is deeply embedded in Serb historic memory and has had crucial significance in the context of the recent conflict in Bosnia-Herzegovina in general and Serb attitude toward today's province of Kosovo in particular. The Battle of Kosovo also marks the beginning of Ottoman rule, which lasted 500 years. Some of the inhabitants in the _region_ of Bosnia were converted to Islam by the occupying Muslim Ottomans, and their descendants are, today, the Bosnian Muslims.

In 1804 there was a Serb uprising against the local Ottoman rulers, the Janissaries who, by this time, also included Bosnian Muslims. This uprising intensified and led to a Serb-Ottoman war. In 1830 the Ottomans granted the Serbs formal autonomy, though the Serbs gained independence from Ottoman rule only in 1878.[4]

After the Ausgleich of 1867 (the 'compromise' between Austria and Hungary that produced the Dual Monarchy), Serbs in the northern section of Serbia, Vojvodina, came under Magyar rule, while the rest of Serbia remained autonomous. In 1918 the Dual Monarchy was dissolved and the Serbs became members of the Kingdom of the Serbs, Croats and Slovenes under the Treaty of St Germain, 1919.

Distinct features that may be factors in a conflict:

Language and script – the Cyrillic script clearly distinguishes the Serbian language from the Croatian which is written in the Latin script. Both languages are versions, or components, of Serbo-Croatian. (In the Conference of Vienna, 1850, participant writers proposed that the Serbo-Croatian language be the basis for a common *nation* of Serbs and Croats.)

Religion – the Eastern Orthodox religion is a bridge between Serbs and Russians; however, it distinguishes Serbs from neighbouring Bosnian and Albanian Muslims, Muslim Bulgarians,[5] Roman Catholic Hungarians, Croats, as well as Slovenes.

History – long-standing military rivalry between Southern Slavs and Magyars, Bulgarians and Greeks. Another salient factor is the memory of the defeat of Orthodox Serbs (or Serbia) by Muslim Turks in the fourteenth century.

Territorial claims – primarily by Serbs in Bosnia where the first Serb 'kingdom', Rascia, was established. There might also be possible territorial claims by Hungary of the now Serbian controlled Vojvodina (inhabited, among others, by Magyars).

The Southern Slav Croats settled in Croatia in the seventh century, accepted Roman Catholic religion in the ninth, formed a kingdom in the tenth and eleventh centuries, and subsequently conquered Dalmatia, on the Adriatic Coast, from the Venetians. Much of the Croatian inhabited regions were conquered in turn by Hungary in 1091. The following year, a union was established between Croatia-Slavonia (as the northern part of Croatia was called) and Hungary under the Hungarian monarch. (In the southern part of later Croatia, Krajina, where the population was mainly Serb, Serb landlords continued to rule.) This union or, from the Croatian side, forced union, lasted for eight centuries, that is, to the end of the nineteenth century.

As Roman Catholics, Croats formed the southern frontier of Christendom. After repulsion of the Ottoman Turks by the Hungarians in 1527, they also formed the southern frontier of the Austro-Hungarian Empire. In the early 1800s there were debates about a Southern Slav unification, but this did not materialise. In the early nineteenth century Magyarisation was introduced in Croatian lands, which prompted Croat reaction in the form of an uprising against Hungarian rule and march into Hungary during the 1848–49 revolution there.

Croatia received independence from Hungary (but not from the Austro-Hungarian Empire) in the 'Sylvester Patent of 1851'. After the 1867 Ausgleich (the Compromise settlement between Austria and Hungary) the Croats received only limited autonomy, which was annulled in 1883. The now independent Croatia, in turn, claimed Bosnia – just freed from Ottoman rule – as an historic part of greater Croatia. Subsequently, the Hungarian government allied with the Serbs in the Krajina region of Croatia against the Croats. In 1918 Croatia became part of the Kingdom of the Serbs, Croats and Slovenes, and later of Yugoslavia.

Distinct features that may be factors in a conflict:
Language and script – affinity between Croat and other Slavic languages in the Balkans but the Latin script distinguishes it from the Serb language.
Religion – the Roman Catholic religion of the Croats creates affinity among Croats and many Hungarians, Slovenians,[6] and Austrians; however, it exacerbates religious schism between them and neighbouring Serbs, Eastern Orthodox and Muslim Bulgarians, and Bosnian and Albanian Muslims.
History – long-standing military rivalry with Hungarians, and of course, the memory of the defeat by Muslim Turks in the sixteenth century and historic memory of perceived domination by Serbs from 1918 on.
Territorial claims – primarily in the northern part of Bosnia and, possibly, in northern Croatia by Hungarians.

The Slovenes – also referred to as 'Alp Slavs' (or Alpine Slavs) migrated to the region of today's Slovenia and parts of today's Austria in the sixth century. The Slovenes, along with other peoples, were subjugated by Charlemagne in 778, and converted to Roman Catholicism. In 843 the Slovenes, who were ruled by a Slovene Duke of Slovene-inhabited Carinthia (now in Austria), were attached to Bavaria which was inhabited primarily by German-speaking peoples. In 1335 both Carinthia and neighbouring Carniola came under the rule of the Habsburgs and were under Austrian rule until 1918. In 1918 Slovenia was included in the Kingdom of Serbs, Croats and Slovenes.

Distinct features that may be factors in a conflict:
Language and script – affinity to other Slavic languages in the Balkans but the Latin script distinguishes them from Serbs – though not from the neighbouring Croats.
Religion – affinity with Catholic Hungarians, Croats, Italians, and Austrians – that is, all their neighbours.
History – historic memory of domination by Austrians (and by Italians, who occupied parts of Slovenia, 1941–45.) No history of confrontation with Ottoman Turks in general, nor Bosnian-Muslims in particular.
Territorial claims – potentially, in the southern part of Austria. On the other hand, potential Italian claims to northern Istria, now forming part of Slovenia.

Bosnians and Herzegovians. Bosnians and Herzegovians of today are the descendants of Serbs, and some Croats, who settled in the seventh century in what became Bosnia in the twelfth century. The Herzegovians lived in a separate duchy called Hum, which was first annexed by Bosnians in the late twelfth century but regained autonomy in the fourteenth century under the name of Herzegovina. The two groups, Bosnians and Herzegovians, continued to live separately until Bosnia fell to the Ottomans in 1463 and Herzegovina in 1482. It was the occupying Ottoman Turks who joined the two groups into one political entity of Bosnia-Herzegovina. The Congress of Berlin (1878) placed Bosnia-Herzegovina under Austro-Hungarian administration. Bosnia-Herzegovina was annexed by the Habsburgs in 1908. In 1918 Bosnia-Herzegovina became part of Serbia which in turn was in the Kingdom of Serbs, Croats and Slovenes.

Distinct features that may be factors in a conflict:
Language and script – Serbo-Croatian language; primarily Latin script.
Religions – Bosnian and Herzegovian Muslims are Muslim, Bosnian Serbs are overwhelmingly Orthodox, and Bosnian Croats are overwhelmingly Roman Catholic.
History – maybe the most important aspect is the various events related to recurrent claims to Bosnia-Herzegovina by both Serbs and Croats.
Territorial claims – probably none.

The Macedonians. According to the Greek version, Macedonians (or Macedons) were Dorian Greeks, not Slavs, who migrated in 1100 BC to the region that was later called Macedonia, while the Slavs arrived in the sixth century and subjugated the Macedonians. According to the Slav or Serb version, ancient Macedons were people who came to what is now northern Greece in the seventh century and subjugated the Slavs who arrived between AD 570 and AD 630. Whatever may be the case, much of the territory of Macedonia came under Ottoman rule in the fourteenth century and so remained until the nineteenth. After the Balkan wars of 1912–14 Macedonia was divided: 51.6 per cent of territory fell in Greece; 38.3 per cent formed Southern Serbia and, after World War II, a republic in Yugoslavia; and 10.1 per cent in Bulgaria.

Distinct features that may be factors in a conflict:
Language and script – Macedonian, with Cyrillic script, was recognised as an official language in 1944 by Tito. (Greeks, Bulgarians consider it a Bulgarian dialect.)
Religion – most Macedonians belong to the Eastern Orthodox Church. In 1964 an Autocephalous Macedonian Church was founded.
History – whatever may be the 'true' history of the people, the over 40 years of existence as an autonomous region within Yugoslavia has created among most inhabitants at least a degree of shared Macedonian identity.
Territorial claims – history of Serb, Bulgarian, Greek and Albanian claims to parts of Macedonia. On the other hand, Macedonians may have claims to territories in all these neighbouring countries.

The Montenegrins. Serbs of the Orthodox faith who formed a principality within Serbia in the fourteenth century. Unlike the rest of Serbia, this principality was not subdued in its entirety by the conquering Ottomans. Between 1515 and 1851 Orthodox bishops ruled in Montenegro. But, in 1715, an alliance was established with the Russian tsars who came to be the spiritual suzerains of the bishops of Montenegro. In 1852 the roles of secular and spiritual rulers separated and at the Congress of Berlin (1878) Montenegro was formally recognised as an independent state. In 1910 Nicholas I proclaimed himself king, Montenegro became a kingdom, participated in the Balkan wars, in the early stages of World War I invaded Albania, and in August 1914 declared war on Austria. In 1915 Montenegro was invaded by Austro-German forces. In 1918 a national assembly deposed Nicholas I and attached Montenegro to Serbia. In 1946 Montenegro was again separated from Serbia, becoming one of the six republics of Yugoslavia.

Distinct features that may be factors in a conflict:
Language and script – Serbian; the script is Cyrillic.
Religion – mostly Eastern Orthodox.
History – Montenegro played an important role first against the Ottomans, then on the Dalmatian coast and with neighbouring Albania. Despite those distinct roles evidence seems to show that Montenegrins consider themselves to be Serbs.
Territorial claims – possibly on the Dalmatian coast.

Northern (Western) Slavs

The Czechs include Czechs in Bohemia (Bohemians) and Moravia (Moravians). In other words, both Bohemians and Moravians are Czechs and their histories are similar. Nevertheless, owing to the prior autonomous existence of Moravia that included Bohemia, and to the more recent nationalist sentiments in Moravia, the two groups, and regions, are at least analytically separable.

The Bohemian Czechs arrived in the region of later Bohemia in the first to fifth centuries. The first Bohemian dynasty was established in the ninth century. From the first to the ninth century, Bohemia constituted a part of the Moravian Empire for a while, and Bohemians accepted Roman Catholicism. St Wenceslaus (920–29), a Bohemian ruler and a Czech national hero, defended the then already autonomous Bohemia against German invasion. Nonetheless, under his brother's rule, Bohemia became an autonomous entity within the Holy Roman Empire in 950.

Moravia, and most of Silesia, were occupied by Bohemia in the early eleventh century and together formed the principality of Bohemia. In 1198 Bohemia became an independent kingdom of the Holy Roman Empire under Ottocar I. The Hussite 'national' and (Protestant) religious rebellion against the (Catholic) Empire erupted in the fifteenth century.

Austrian, Habsburg, rule had begun in 1526. Bohemia lost its autonomy, and the Jesuits were introduced to the region by the Habsburgs in order to return Bohemians to Roman Catholicism. After years of Protestant versus Catholic confrontation, religious freedom was introduced in 1609. In 1618 King Matthias cancelled religious freedom (granted in the Letter of Majesty), the Bohemian diet revolted, and threw two imperial councillors out of a window. This act, called the 'Defenestration of Prague' (fenestra, window in Latin) started the Thirty Year War. In the battle of the White Mountain (1620) the Bohemian Protestants were defeated and in 1627 Bohemia was demoted from being a constituent Habsburg 'kingdom' to become an imperial 'crown land'.

The Peace of Westphalia (1648) brought to Bohemian-Czech lands intensive Germanisation that continued to the mid-nineteenth century. In 1848 a Slavic Congress gathered in Prague under the leadership of Frantisek Palacky, a Czech national hero, but in 1849 Austrian rule was restored. When the Austrian-Hungarian Dual Monarchy was created (1867), the Bohemian lands were not granted an independent status but were relegated to be a province of the Empire. Although some concessions were made in 1879, independence came to Czechoslovakia only in 1919.

Distinct features that may be factors in a conflict:
Language and script – Czech language; Latin script.
Religion – Czechs are either nominally Roman Catholic or nominally Protestant.

History – probably the most significant elements in past history are, the Hussite rebellion (15th century); Habsburg-Austrian rule (1526–1919); and the gaining of independence as Czechoslovakia (1919).
Territorial claims – arguably, alongside borders between Bohemia and Germany and Poland.

The Moravians. The Great Moravian Empire was formed in the ninth century which, for varying lengths of time, included Bohemia, Silesia, Slovakia, parts of today's southern Poland, and northern Hungary. In the ninth century they, the same as the Bohemians, accepted the Roman Catholic faith. In 894 the Moravian Empire reached its zenith under Svatopluk, but by the early tenth century Moravia was under Hungarian rule. In 955 Otto I, of the Holy Roman Empire, defeated the Hungarians and Moravia became part of the Holy Roman Empire together with Bohemia. The Kingdom of Moravia came under Austrian rule in 1526 along with Bohemia; however, Moravia was separate from Bohemian rule for various periods of time. In reaction to the Bohemian revolt of the White Mountain the Habsburgs subjugated the Moravians as well. In 1849 Bohemians and Moravians demanded to be unified, but Moravia was made an Austrian crownland. In 1919 Moravia was incorporated into Czechoslovakia.

Distinct features that may be factors in a conflict:
History – long history as an independent entity.
Territorial claims – arguably, alongside border with Germany.

The Slovaks are closely related to the Czechs linguistically and ethnically. However, the Czechs and Slovaks have had a separate cultural and political life for much of the last thousand years.

Slovaks settled in the region of today's Slovakia in the fifth and sixth centuries. In the ninth century they, and the Czechs, were part of the Kingdom of Moravia, where they also accepted the Roman Catholic religion. However, the Slovaks, but not the Czechs, came under Hungarian rule in the tenth century. In the fourteenth century Czech-Slovak contacts were renewed and by the fifteenth century the Hussite rebellion had influence among some Slovaks. When Hungary fell under Ottoman occupation in 1526, Slovaks, along with western Hungary, came under Habsburg rule. Ottoman occupation ended in the seventeenth century. Apart from this relatively short period Slovaks were under Hungarian rule from the tenth century until Czechoslovakia's independence in 1919.

Educated Slovaks in the political forefront tended to be members of the Catholic clergy. They were the ones who, under the leadership of Ludovit Stur, presented demands in 1848 to the Habsburg rulers for greater autonomy. The demand was rejected. After the founding of the Dual Monarchy (1867), Slovaks remained under exclusive Hungarian rule and Magyarisation intensified. Between 1900–10 large numbers of landless Slovak peasants migrated to the United States. On 1 October 1918 the Slovak National Council voted for independence from Hungary and joined Czechoslovakia.

Distinct features that may be factors in a conflict:
Religion – primarily Roman Catholic, and Protestant.
History – almost a thousand year long Hungarian rule which harbours animosity; ambivalent relations with Czechs.
Territorial claims – alongside the border with Hungary and, to a degree, with the Czech Republic.

The Lusatians descended from the Slavic Wends (or Sorbs) and are also called Lusatian Sorbs. Their number is estimated between 50,000 to about 300,000, most of them in the region where Germany meets the south-west Polish border. The Lusatians are divided into two groups on the basis of their language: Upper Lusatian, closer to the Czech Republic of today, and Lower Lusatian nearer to the Polish border.

The conquest of the region of Lusatia by Germans began in the eighth century, completed by Charlemagne, and, in the tenth century, formed into *margravates* of Upper and Lower Lusatia. The forceful conversion of the animist Lusatians to Christianity started at the beginning of the twelfth century and ended by the beginning of the thirteenth. In the Treaty of Prague (1635) Lusatia was given to Saxony, and in the Congress of Vienna (1815) Lower Lusatia and part of Upper Lusatia were attached to Prussia. Most Lusatians assimilated as Czechs in independent Czechoslovakia.[7]

Distinct features that may be factors in a conflict:
Religion – Roman Catholic, while many of their neighbours are nominally so.
History – being a relatively small minority and part of various political arrangements.
Territorial claims – none.

Ruthenians. The name Ruthenian may be a Latinized version of 'Russian'. The name was applied during the existence of Austria-Hungary to the inhabitants of western Ukraine, and also to groups of people in Galicia, Bukovina and Carpathian Ukraine. After the dissolution of Austria-Hungary in 1918 and the independence of Czechoslovakia the next year, the term referred only to the inhabitants of eastern-most part of Czechoslovakia, in the Carpathian mountains. Often the names Ruthenian, Carpatho-Ukrainian, Subcarpathian Rus-Ruthenian were used interchangeably. For example, the only apparent distinction between some Ukrainians and Ruthenians was that the majority of the latter were members of the Ruthenian Uniate Church (since the sixteenth century), while the majority of the former were members, since the seventeenth century, of the Greek Orthodox Church.

Distinct features that may be factors in a conflict:
Religion – Ruthenian Uniate, thus different from the religions of the peoples among whom they live.
History – never formed an independent political entity but sections of the population seem to claim a separate national identity.
Territorial claims – possible claims by Ukrainians to the region of Slovakia where Ruthenians live.

THE GERMAN-SPEAKING PEOPLES

We shall mention the German-speaking peoples as a whole, then the German-speaking Austrians and some of the German-speaking minorities in Central European regions under consideration, particularly German speakers in the Sudetes and in Silesia.
The peoples generally referred to as 'Germans' first inhabited the

regions of today's North Germany, Denmark, southern Sweden and the shores of the Baltic Sea. From there they spread from the seventh century BC to other parts of Europe to form a large circle that ranges from Iceland, to Scotland, to central France, northern Italy, Austria, Norway and back to Iceland. German-speaking 'tribes' migrated in the fourth and fifth centuries AD south and eastward, conquered major parts of the Roman Empire and faced, across the Elbe River, the Slavic-speaking peoples. In about the sixth century, Slavic-speaking peoples conquered Styria, Carinthia and lower Austria. In AD 788 Charlemagne set up the first Austrian March (Austrian borderland, or Osterreich) against the invading Avars in today's Lower and Upper Austria.

After Charlemagne's death in 814 the Austrian March fell to the Moravians then to the Magyars. However, in 955 Otto I reinstated the Austrian March and attached it to Bavaria while Otto II bestowed it on Leopold of Babenberg who founded the first Austrian dynasty, the Habsburg dynasty.

The Habsburgs were originally a landowning family who took their name from a castle near the Swiss border in the tenth or eleventh century. Subsequently members of the family inherited more lands, married into ruling families of neighbouring lands or conquered other lands (and their inhabitants), and thus enlarged their holdings. In other words, land was the basis of their power. Bohemian and Hungarian Estates (electoral bodies) and Croatia's ruler (the former in 1526, the latter in 1527) elected to be part of the Habsburg holdings, and the character of the realm and position of the Habsburg monarchy changed. It became an Empire composed of culturally, ethnically different entities; it became multiethnic or multinational. After the Peace of Westphalia (1648), the Austrian Habsburg Empire gradually replaced the Holy Roman Empire in importance.

Germans in the Austro-Hungarian Empire

Roman Catholic German peasants and traders were sent by Maria Theresa and her son, Joseph II of the Habsburgs (1765–90), to the eastern parts of the Austro-Hungarian Empire in order to reduce excess population in Austria. The prospective settlers were granted travel expenses and promised religious freedom in their new countries. Some 17,000 settled among Catholic Croats and Hungarians in the Backa and the Banat regions between 1784–87. They learned Hungarian and served in the Hungarian army in World War I. In 1842 an estimated 1,200,000 Germans resided in the Hungarian crownlands.

Germans in Sudetes

The Sudetes (Sudeten in German) is a mountain range between Bohemia and Poland. It has been inhabited by Germans, who began to settle there and elsewhere in the Bohemian kingdom in the twelfth and thirteenth centuries. There was a decline in the number of Germans during the Hussite Wars, but by the sixteenth century their numbers grew. In the eighteenth century German became the official language in Bohemia which Czechs resisted then and throughout the nineteenth century.

HUNGARIANS (OR MAGYARS)

The Magyars, a Finno-Ugric people originating from beyond the Ural mountains, migrated to the region of today's Hungary and Transylvania in the ninth century. The Hungarian kingdom started to solidify under the first Hungarian King St Stephan (1001–38) who brought about the Christianisation of the population. King Bela III (1172–96) started to grant privileges to a few landowning Hungarian nobles, the magnates, while the lesser nobles, peasants and towns-people had virtually none. Under pressure from lesser nobles, the Golden Bull, the 'Magna Carta of Hungary' was granted in 1222, limiting the power of the nobles and established the beginnings of a parliament. In 1241 the country was occupied by Mongols for a year.

Hungary's borders have changed over the centuries. But, overall, Hungary's boundaries included, in the north, a large Slovak population, in Transylvania a large Romanian population and, in the Balkans, Croatian, and for shorter periods, Serb and Bosnian populations.

In 1526 the Ottoman Turks defeated the Hungarians at Mohacs. Subsequently, Hungary split into three parts: a narrow western part of the country was ruled by Austrian and Hungarian nobles; a central part, including the capital, came completely under Turkish domination; and Transylvania came under the rule of Hungarian nobles. In 1683 the Ottoman Turks laid siege to Vienna and some Hungarian nobles, opposing the Austrians, assisted the Turks. But the Austrians repulsed the Turks, and in 1686 liberated Budapest from Ottoman rule. In 1687 Hungarian nobles accepted Austrian rule over Hungary and in 1699 Turkey ceded all of Hungary and Transylvania to the Austrians in the Peace of Kalowitz. The Transylvanian Hungarian nobility continued to fight the Austrians, but in 1711 they were defeated. In 1718 the Austrians took the Banat too (see below).

From the late eighteenth century on the Austrians brought into Hungary many Germans, as well as Slavs, and Joseph II aspired to a complete Germanisation of Hungary (see above).

The *Banat* is a frontier region in what was southern Hungary, western Transylvania, and eastern Croatia. The word 'Banat' means: ruled by *bans* (local governors). Slavs settled there in the fifth and Hungarians in the ninth centuries. In 1233 it was established as a Hungarian frontier province. In 1552, after many Serbs escaped to what was named the Banat from Ottoman wars, it became a Turkish *sanjak* (province). In 1718 it was made an Austrian military frontier, as the Banat of Temesvar. Between 1779–1918 the Banat belonged to Hungary.

Vojvodina was part of Hungary and Croatia when, in the sixteenth century, it was overrun by the Ottomans. It was restored to Hungary in 1699 and ceded to Yugoslavia in the Treaty of Trianon (1920). Vojvodina was inhabited by Hungarians, as well as eighteenth century refugee Croats, Serbs, German colonists, Romanians and Slovaks. The three regions of Vojvodina are: (a) the Srem, in the south-west, which was part of Croatia and Slavonia until 1918; (b) Backa, in the north-west, which was formerly part of Hungary; and (c) the western part of the Banat of Temesvar.

*

We have completed the sketchy overview of the degree and scope of ethnic diversity in Central Europe and highlighted events which may have been particularly relevant to the formation of that diversity. The resulting picture is incomplete. Not only are the descriptions provided partial, but also we have not included each and every group. Our main purpose was to outline the ethnic mosaic and to assist in grasping its scope. Our secondary, and rather implicit, purpose was to lay the ground for our subsequent discussion of ethnic conflict. We wish to emphasise, however, that the connection between ethnic diversity and ethnic conflict may be more apparent than real. True, if and where an ethnic difference exists, a division between 'us' and 'them' is already present. However, our basic tenet is that ethnic diversity itself does not produce conflict. It is only that it is exploitable and, too frequently, has been exploited to produce ethnic conflict.

NOTES

1. Although Hungarian and Magyar will at times be used interchangeably (Hungarian is a foreign term for Magyar), we shall try to use 'Hungary' or 'Hungarian' in reference to the country and 'Magyar' in reference to a person or people.
2. There is additional division between groups of people who use Latin script; others use Cyrillic scripts.
3. We refer to the Slav linguistic group which, for the sake of brevity, will be called Slavs, or Slavic peoples. We shall also use 'Germans', or 'German people', instead of the 'German linguistic group', and so on.
4. It is relevant to note here that one observer, L.P. Meriage, convincingly argues that the 1804 rebellion was not a nationalist uprising but a provincial affair of Serbs around Belgrade. According to Meriage, national unification and independence were not issues to the Serbs dispersed throughout the Balkans until the late nineteenth and early twentieth century. L.P. Meriage, 'The First Serbian Uprising (1804–1813): National Revival or a Search for Regional Security', *Canadian Review of Studies in Nationalism*, 4, 2 (Spring 1977), pp. 187–205. Likewise, the so-called 'Greek liberation war' 1821–30 also began as a rebellion of small groups, the 'Kleftes', and turned into a war of independence later.
5. Julian Konstantinov, 'An Account of Pomak Conversions in Bulgaria', in G. Seewann, ed., *Minderheitenfragen in Sudost-Europa* (Munich: Oldenburg, 1992), pp. 343–58.
6. Slovenes and Slovenians is used interchangeably.
7. After World War II, the Lusatians sought but did not attain recognition as a nation, though they were recognised as an ethnic minority by the German Democratic Republic.

2 Response to diversity – prior to World War I

In this chapter we focus in two sections on the plight of ethnic groups – or nationalities – prior to World War I. In Section I, the focus is on the Ottoman Empire and in Section II on the Austro-Hungarian Empire, that is, the period before the Ausgleich of 1867, and on the Austrian-Hungarian Dual Monarchy, the period after 1867. The period between the two world wars will be dealt with in Chapter 3, and the post-World War II period in Chapter 4.

I. IN THE OTTOMAN EMPIRE

The Muslim Ottoman Turks, originally an ethnic entity in what is today's Anatolia in Turkey, first conquered neighbouring peoples; then, from the fourteenth century, they spread to the Balkans. In 1453 Constantinople was conquered. Bosnia and Herzegovina were annexed in 1465. In 1526 the Ottoman Turks defeated the Hungarians at Mohacs and conquered almost all of Hungary and Transylvania. However, they did not succeed in their conquest of a section of western Hungary already under Habsburg occupation. This strip of land served the Hungarian dynasty as their domain for the next 200 years and from there to pursue a legitimate claim to the rest of the country. Their opposition to the Ottoman conquest enabled other rulers as well in Central Europe to consolidate their rule.

The Millet System
Ottoman rulers controlled a wide variety of peoples for centuries by force and other means, and had a great impact on political formations,

religion and other aspects of public life in all the lands and peoples they conquered.

Under Sultan Orhan, the Ottomans had introduced in 1453 a system of rule in the Near East and the Balkans, the millet system, which allowed autonomy for non-Turkic and non-Muslim groups. A millet was 'a community or nation of people with a particular religion within the Ottoman Empire'.[1] Members of the millet had the right to use their own language, to have their own religious, cultural and educational institutions, and a leader responsible for all public affairs of the millet. There were three millets for several non-Turkic and non-Muslim groups: for Christian, Armenian and Jewish groups. In addition to these three millets, there was also a fourth, Muslim millet, for non-Ottoman Muslims.

The three original millets, Orthodox, Armenian and Jewish, underwent reorganisation in 1862–66. The patriarchs (heads) and the *synods* (councils) became elected by members of the community in the Orthodox and the Armenian millets. More and more of the elected members of the synod were traders, or otherwise non-religious elements, who came to deal with secular matters. The patriarch, in turn, dealt with religious affairs. Also, by the nineteenth century new millets were created. Serbian, Bulgarian and Romanian communities became separate millets under their separate churches and, gradually, more and more as separate nations. Serbians were under the Greek Orthodox millet but were permitted to organise either under their own church, or around their own ethnic-linguistic organisation. The Greeks, for their part, established their own Orthodox church separate from the patriarch of Istanbul. Converted Muslim-Bosnians and Muslim-Albanians could preserve their separate ethnic-linguistic identity in addition to, or rather than, the Muslim one.

There were also groups of foreigners in the Ottoman realm organised in 'national' millets, whose status was affixed according to formal treaties between the foreign government and the Sultan. The existence of 'national' millets may have been instrumental in making available – this phrase is used advisedly – a national identity alongside communal and religious identities.

The original national millets were of Venetians, Florentines, Genoese, and others. But more and more missionaries of various denominations arrived in the Ottoman, which is to say Muslim, lands, who needed protection and specific rights. These missionaries secured protection and rights from their respective governments – particularly the Russian, the French, and the British. Even though missionaries, *qua* missionaries, could not form a millet, French Catholics, or English Protestants, for example, could. Consequently, the various foreign governments supported their nationals under the guise of supporting religious millets. Thus in 1850 a Protestant millet was recognised through the efforts of the British Ambassador to Turkey, Sir Stratford de Redcliffe. Overall, the French government supported (French) Catholics, the Russians the (Serb) Orthodox, and the British the (English) Protestants.

This considerable interchangeability between nationality and religion evolved through time. Nonetheless, Muslims everywhere under Ottoman rule remained in a separate category. Kemal Karpat has noted:

> In the early censuses, beginning in the fifteenth and sixteenth centuries, the non-Muslim citizens were classified as Christian, Armenian, and Jewish. . . . In the second half of the nineteenth century the Christians began to be classified into ethno confessional categories – for example, Bulgarians, Maronites, Syriacs. However, throughout the existence of the Ottoman state, in all censuses, the Muslims were listed as one group and never categorised according to ethnic or linguistic differences.[2]

The millet system was not the only administrative innovation introduced by the Ottoman rulers. There was, for example, the system of capitulations.

Capitulations

Originally, capitulations were special trading rights granted by the Ottomans to foreign nationals in the Ottoman Empire. They were designed to encourage foreign trade, and were worded and signed by representatives of foreign governments within the Ottoman government.

By the nineteenth century capitulations had become a significant institution in several ways. First, foreign nationals had gained considerable influence in the Turkish economy. Second, Turkish subjects found ways to become foreigners in their own country and to acquire rights that capitulations provided. This could be done by obtaining from a foreign Embassy or Consulate a document called the *barat* which made that Ottoman subject also a national of that foreign country. Through the barat, Turkish subjects, and their descendants, could become foreign nationals and enjoy the rights and protection that such a status provided. This allowed privileges for many. For example, foreign nationals did not pay local taxes, could not be tried in Turkish courts, and could not be arrested by Turkish police.

Response to Diversity

Two questions are of especial interest to us here. The first question is whether the millet system and, possibly additional measures, helped to prevent conflict – particularly ethnic conflict – in the Ottoman Empire? One might add here, that we are not referring to the numerous internal and external wars that the Ottomans waged but only to conflict, primarily ethnic conflict, among 'peoples', that is, ethnic groups, within the Empire.

There is no complete answer to this question because one cannot know if conflicts would have erupted if no millet system had been erected. One might surmise however, that the system may have been one factor reducing the likelihood of conflict. Millets were self-ruling autonomous, though not sovereign, communities with relatively homogeneous populations sharing a language, ethnic origin, often a religion. Heads and representative bodies were elected from within the millets. Intervention in the internal affairs of millets by the Ottoman rulers was minimal. As millets were often also geographically separate from each other, contact and competition among them – for political offices, spheres of jurisdiction – was kept at minimum.

The second question is even more complex. It is whether the millet system, introduced as a method of merely administering diverse populations, had become eventually a base for the *national* consciousness of various ethnic groups. Also in this regard, and in retrospect, did the granting of autonomy to self-ruling communities – and the possible national identity that might have emerged within

them – lead to subsequent *national* awakening and demand for
sovereign independence? Still in the same context, did the various
other measures that may be regarded as components of a process
of modernisation, contribute to, or even bring about, national
aspirations?

In responding to these questions, one factor should be taken into
consideration. The millet system was introduced long before the
French Revolution and thus well before the recognition of peoples'
rights. True, many reforms of the system were introduced in the
nineteenth century, after the French Revolution. It may be then that
not the introduction of the millet system but its later reforms should
be considered as a factor in the emergence of a national spirit or
consciousness. One might also take into consideration that at its
base, the millet system was an administrative system, a method of
rule, and might be seen as a version of 'indirect rule' which was
practised by colonial rulers in other parts of the world. Whether
or not 'indirect rule' was instrumental in national awakening is
debatable.

It may be fair to assume that reforms introduced in the Ottoman
Empire after the French Revolution were not the offspring of
Enlightenment ideas. The historian Sheldon Fisher notes, and there
seems to be sufficient evidence to underline it, that:

> [t]he reforms of Mahmud II [born 1785; ruled 1808–1839] were
> conceived not so much in the spirit of the French Revolution and
> eighteenth century enlightenment as in the pattern of governmental
> changes enacted by Louis XIV and Napoleon Bonaparte to strengthen
> and widen the authority of the central regime.[3]

For example, in order to bring about greater centralisation,
Mahmud II abolished the *Janissaries*, a military institution, whose
members were recruited from among the various peoples conquered
by the Ottomans. Thus, an Albanian could be a Janissar, hence
an important person, in the Ottoman hierarchy. However, the
demobilised Janissaries were capable and ready to organise an army
after the decline of the Empire.

But Fisher's comment may not be applicable to Mahmud II's son,
Abdul Mejid, who succeeded him in 1839 and under whom Reshid

Pasha, his Foreign Minister, introduced many new reforms. In 1845 Reshid initiated *Tanzimat*, 'a movement for reorganisation along the lines of pure and tolerant Muslim practices'.[4] These were reforms in many spheres. Local assemblies were established, courts were reformed. Law, diplomacy, administration were modernised. A major effort was put into education. The University of Istanbul was established in 1846 and secondary education was reformed by the 1850s. Inevitably, education led to the growth of an educated strata and to the publication of books and newspapers. Reforms were aimed also at non-Muslims which implied a process of secularisation. Fisher notes that '... the idea [of] Ottomanism, promising equality for all subjects, was beginning to have a sizable following'.[5] After the Crimean War (1856), a new document was issued, the Hatt-i Humayun (Imperial Rescript) which provided equality to the Christian population of the Empire. Each millet could now choose an assembly, and religion was no longer an obstacle to enter any school, hold public office, or enter the army. There were additional reforms in virtually all spheres of public life

All this does not mean that the political regime of the Ottoman Empire was becoming democratic. Far from it. But few regimes in Europe were democratic in the 1850s. Universal suffrage was not introduced even in Great Britain until after World War I. Nevertheless, inhabitants of the Ottoman Empire – Serbs, Bosnians, Hungarians and others – enjoyed liberties that many other populations enjoyed in many other parts of Europe of the period, in principle and, far less, in practice.

With all this said and taken into account, there seems to be no clear-cut evidence that either the millet system, the tanzimat, and/or other reforms – which may be included under 'modernisation' – brought about the rise of a national spirit. Even if modernisation may be counted as a factor, one could point to several other factors that brought about rebellions in the Balkans, the independence of several states there, and to the eventual end of Ottoman rule for all by 1918.

One such possible factor was the fluctuating and eventually declining effectiveness of Ottoman power over the various peoples in the faraway lands of the Empire. The weakness of Ottoman power meant the lack of immediate effective response to local insurrections against the Ottoman Turks, which then got out of hand.

Another, related, factor was the opposition of the traditional
Muslim rulers to Mahmud's reforms in Bosnia. Under their leadership, Bosnians rebelled in 1831 and again in 1848. They were subdued
in 1850 by Omar Pasha, a Croat by birth, who established Sarajevo as
Bosnia's capital. Then, there were the occasional open revolts in
Bosnia-Herzegovina in reaction to taxation by Montenegrins and
Serbs. In the 1860s and 1870s the Ottoman regime tried to avoid
virtual bankruptcy by raising taxes. Indeed, open revolt in Bosnia
and Herzegovina erupted in earnest in 1875, and that too mainly in
opposition to taxation. Montenegrins and Serbs, on their part,
declared war in July 1876 in support of the Bosnians. The Russian
Tsar also supported the Bosnians and the Serbs, which led to the
eventual involvement of Britain as well.

Still another possible factor was the rivalry among rulers of the
main European powers of the time, who lent support to 'minority
groups' within their rivals' empires. In 1820 in Greece, for example,
there were rebellions against local rulers. In 1821, Ottoman troops
came in to repress an insurrection called for by the Greek prince
Alexandros Ypsilanti; the invasion brought about a general Greek
revolt. A Greek massacre of Muslims was followed, in retaliation, by
a Turkish Ottoman massacre of Christians. The main European
powers, including Russia, supporting 'human rights and nationalist
spirit', pressed Istanbul not to further repress the defiant Greeks,
and Greece was granted independence in 1830.

An Assessment

The Ottoman rulers, instead of destroying or trying to assimilate the
various religious and ethnic entities in the Balkans, recognised them
and organised them into the millet system, thus providing them with
a degree of political identity. Yet that identity, gained through the
millet system in the nineteenth century, was not enough to lead to
demands for independent statehood. Karpat points to a very important
consideration in regard to the Arab Middle East which is relevant to
the Balkans as well:

> ... both the concept of the territorial state and that of the nation-state
> as the West understands it ... remain alien to the [Middle-East's]
> historical experience, its political culture, and its idea of community.[6]

In the Arab Middle East, and the Balkans, community is 'the concrete organisation expression of ethno religious identity and solidarity'.[7] Boundaries of a community are not important for members of a community. Community can be, and perceived by its members as, a political organisation, a political unit, but without being a territorially defined entity. Karpat argues that:

> ... the sense of identity and solidarity in all the Middle Eastern 'national' states derives to a large extent from their sense of religious identity and communality instead of from feelings of ethnic and/or linguistic group solidarity.[8]

And further:

> Regardless of the different ethnopolitical labels under which these 'national states' are presented today, the citizens' sense of identity is nurtured psychologically, largely by the old communal identities.[9]

We might infer from all the above, that the various peoples in the Balkans would not by themselves have claimed sovereignty within bordered territories of a state, because they already lived in autonomous political communities, the millets, providing them with a 'sense of identity and solidarity'. They did follow secular and religious leaders in opposing taxation and reforms. But the idea that they needed a territorial state, a sovereign state recognised by foreign governments, had to come from the outside.

And it did. It was Western governments that promoted the notion of the territorial state. And they did that not for the sake of modernisation; they wished to weaken the Ottoman empire, or in any case gain greater influence in the Balkans, and for these purposes they entered into diplomatic relations with governments, signed treaties with them and prompted them to declare wars. The Western notion of 'territorial state' had a considerable impact particularly among educated Orthodox-Christian Serbs, who used that Western notion in their fight against Ottoman rule. The least one can say is that Western governments effected the change of communities into territorial states, because such a change meant an effective weakening of Ottoman rule in a region towards which they harboured strategic designs.

Of course, Western powers were assisted in this regard by Westernised elites in the Ottoman Empire, the products of modernisation in general and education in particular. Already the missionaries, who had little success in conversion, brought with them Western notions and ideas. Then, the 1848 revolutions had some impact in the Ottoman Empire; educational reforms introduced produced an educated elite. The Young Turks of the 1908 revolution in Turkey did absorb democratic *ideas* and *ideals* in the later part of the nineteenth century and at the beginning of the twentieth. The educated started to think in Western political terms. What the educated have learned, first, is political terminology, and then the possible connections among such terms. Fisher remarks, for example, that one Namik Kamal, a member of the Turkish Patriotic Alliance, formed in 1865, made the words 'freedom' and 'fatherland' popular in Istanbul.[10]

With the weakening of the Ottoman Empire, and especially after the Revolution of the Young Turks against Ottoman rule in 1908 – when Ottomanisation or Turkification became the political slogan – non-Turkic rebellion in the Empire also intensified. By that time, in the early twentieth century, 'nation', 'freedom', 'nationalism', and 'fatherland' could only be realised in Western terms. Clearly, the major Empires of the day, the British, the French with their colonies, and imperial Russia, could not serve as models for modern states. But the emerging states of Germany, Italy and, to a degree Austria and Hungary, members of a newly reformed Dual Monarchy, could – and probably did. Thus, in the final account, Western interests in the Balkans and the ideas of the educated strata did complement each other.

One additional point may be worthy of mentioning here. After the Young Turk Rebellion of 1908, the new Turkish governments aimed at the reorganisation of the *Empire* as a centrally administered Turkish unitary state. The key term here is 'centralisation'. Such a reorganisation, in turn, was opposed by the Western-influenced non-Turkic elites who – being encouraged by Western powers – promoted the idea of having their own independent states.

In sum, it is true that rebellions had erupted in the Ottoman Empire from the beginning of the nineteenth century. But 'nationalist' rebellions in the Balkans occurred after 1908. The Albanian rebellion erupted in 1911 and the Young Turk government recognised their independence in 1912. The First Balkan War – Bulgaria, Greece, Serbia v. the Ottoman Empire – was waged from October 1912 to May 1913. (Treaty of London, 30 May 1913.) The Second Balkan War, among the newly independent states, in 1913, ended with the Treaty of Bucharest, August 1913.

Ultimately, we can *not* say for certain that the millet system did not or could not function as a practical means of resolving conflicts in the multiethnic framework of the Ottoman Empire. We do know that Turkey's loss of its European Empire, the Balkans and beyond, is due more to the weakness of the Turkish regime and its attempt to centralise the Empire than to the strength of the aspiration among the millet populations in the Empire to live in Western type national-states. What we also know is that intra-Balkan national and ethnic wars erupted after the loosely called nation-states emerged there. With all this said, one might also mention that some Serbs have always dreamed – without necessarily thinking of a territorial state – of revenging the defeat in Kosovo in 1389, and re-establishing a 'Serb Empire'. What conclusions one should draw from all this, we shall leave as an open question for the moment.

II. IN THE AUSTRO-HUNGARIAN EMPIRE

Both the challenges of and responses to 'ethnicity' were considerably different in the Austrian and Hungarian realms from those in the Ottoman Empire. Geographic location might provide one explanation of that difference. Austria, and to a lesser degree Hungary, were close to Western Europe where the ideas that brought about the spirit of independence had originated. There was no significant Islamic conversion in the Austro-Hungarian Empire. The ethnic and religious mosaic was also different in the two regions. One may enumerate other differences. Nevertheless, the challenge of 'ethnicity' was no less intensive in the Austrian and Hungarian holdings than in the Ottoman Empire; maybe even more so. One possible explanation for the similarity of the ethnic challenge may be that in both regions ethnic groups were and felt dominated by 'others'. In the Ottoman Empire, Orthodox Christians by Muslims, for example; in the Austro-Hungarian Empire, Slavic language speakers by Magyars, Magyars by Austrians. The greater exposure to relevant Western ideas in Austria-Hungary may explain the possible greater intensity of the challenge there.

Most of the major ethnic groups have already been listed in Chapter 1. Nonetheless, it seems useful to provide here a list pertaining only to the Austro-Hungarian Empire and, at the same time, to present these groups from a new perspective.

The principal Austro-Hungarian 'national groups' were, in alphabetical order: Croats, Czechs, Germans, Italians, Magyars, Poles, Romanians, Ruthenians, Serbs, Slovaks, Slovenes.

We may group them by linguistic factors: Northern Slavs: Czechs, Slovaks, Poles, Ruthenians. Southern Slavs: Slovenes, Croats, Serbs. 'Latins': Italians. Romanians; Germans; Magyars.

We may group them by country: in the Austrian (dominantly German linguistic) part of the Dual Monarchy: Czechs (Bohemians and Moravians), Slovenes and Germans, and a small number of Italians and Poles. That is: four Northern Slavs, one Latin and one German.

In the Hungarian (dominantly Magyar linguistic) part of the Dual Monarchy: Croats, Romanians, Ruthenians, Serbs, and Slovaks. That is: two Northern Slavs, two Southern Slavs, one Latin.

In other words, in the Austrian part of the monarchy there were only three major groups (four, if we consider Bohemians and Moravians separately), in the Hungarian part of the monarchy, on the other hand, there were five.

RESPONSE TO DIVERSITY PRIOR TO 1867

Our narrative will follow chronologically and focus only on the factors relevant to our topic. The early days have already been noted: the Austrian Habsburg dynasty, originally a landowning family, took their name from a castle in the Swiss canton Aargau in the tenth or eleventh century. Subsequently, members of the family conquered other lands (and peoples on them), and thus enlarged their holdings which, initially, were part of the Holy Roman Empire. Rudolph I (1273–91) was the first Habsburg Emperor.

The Emperors of the Holy Roman Empire were elected by the Estates (electoral bodies) – who were the representatives of the various feudal holdings – and then crowned by the Pope in Rome. When the Bohemian and Hungarian Estates and Croatia's ruler (the former in 1526, the latter in 1527) chose to be part of the Habsburg holdings and signed treaties to that effect, the Habsburg Empire came into existence. The Habsburg Empire became multiethnic in the sixteenth century.

Holding the Empire together was not easy. The Hungarian aristocracy wanted to free themselves from Habsburg domination as early as the sixteenth century and some sought out the Ottoman Turks as allies in their desire. The Thirty Year War broke out partly to prevent the Bohemian aristocracy's breakaway. The 'Pragmatic Sanction' of Charles VI (1713), establishing the rights of succession of Habsburg rulers, was to ensure, and did ensure for a while, the integrity of the Empire. However questionable the 'Pragmatic Sanction' seemed to be in the eyes of Hungarian, Bohemian and probably other nobilities and landowners – the only ones who counted in the early eighteenth century – it was institutionalised into a system of rule. In the early part of the eighteenth century, the Habsburg Empire was at its zenith and provided a framework for the ethnic groups contained in it, most of them composed of landless and uneducated peasants.

Nevertheless, the 'Pragmatic Sanction' proved an inadequate response to demands that started to be presented 'from below', from within the ethnic mosaic, when these demands surfaced after the French Revolution of 1789. They erupted in the Revolutions of 1848. These developments will be briefly surveyed here.

The Congress of Vienna

The Congress of Vienna of 1815, a gathering of leading statesmen of the time, was to respond to the demands that the impact of the French Revolutionary ideas produced and, more concretely, to the changes that the Napoleonic Wars had effected. For example, after defeating the Prussian army, Napoleon created the Duchy of Warsaw, and liberated territories and peoples formerly under Prussian as well as Austrian rule.

Those convening in the Congress of Vienna after Napoleon's defeat, aimed at restoring the old order in Europe as much as possible.

One of its tasks was to reallocate territories affected by the Napoleonic wars. Indeed, Russia (under Tsar Alexander) got part of Poland as well as Finland; Austria received Galicia and parts of later Italy: the Venetian Republic, the Duchy of Milan, Tuscany, Parma and Modena; and Prussia received Posen and the corridor of Danzig (Gdansk). One of the erudite intellectuals later wrote that 'if the reader will look at the map of Europe as the Congress of Vienna drew it, he will see that this gathering seems almost as if it had planned the maximum of local exasperation'.[11]

The author was H.G. Wells, the book was *The Outline of History*, the Congress of Vienna took place in 1815, and the date of the book's publication was 1920. In any case, to safeguard Christianity, justice and peace and to control in the future any outburst of 'disorder' within these Empires – including ethnic conflicts and nationalist manifestations – the Quadruple Alliance was formed (among the rulers of Austria, Prussia, Russia and Great Britain), which later was re-formed into the Holy Alliance (without Great Britain).

Attempted 'Solutions' – 1815–48

The main figure in this period was Metternich, Chancellor of Austria 1815–48, who took as his mission to repress all manifestations of the ideas of the French Revolution and all manifestations of 'liberalism'. He strengthened censorship, oversaw control of education by clerics, investigated plots against the regime by a variety of means, and launched police raids on suspected students. His 'Carlsbad Decrees' forbade the granting of any constitution in the Empire which would contradict the principles of the monarchy.

These practical 'solutions' did not stop the discontent which was already gathering nationalist undertones. Secret societies were formed and there were a few organised rebellions. Also, various 'liberal' groups emerged in several regions of the Habsburg Empire – and beyond – which, in turn, affected the Empire either directly or indirectly. For example, there were 'disturbances' in what later became Germany and Italy; the Austrians were invited to restore order. The first half of the nineteenth century were the decades of the 'gathering storm'. In Russia the 'Decembrists' tried, but failed, to promote a liberal government after the death of Tsar Alexander in 1825. In Spain French troops came to repress a rebellion; Portugal lost its colonial holding in Brazil, which became independent in 1822. As previously mentioned, the Greek revolt in the Ottoman Empire was, in the eyes of Metternich, a rebellion against a 'legitimate sovereign', the Ottomans. In Central Europe, Poles rose against the Tsar Nicolas in 1830, but he crushed them the following year.

It seems appropriate to mention here in passing the Age of Romanticism which roughly overlapped the waves of rebellion and uprisings, but which had little if any effect in the Ottoman Empire, except among Serbs. The central features of Romanticism were the glorification of the individual and the veneration of nature. Among the better known Romanticists were, in literature, Wordsworth and Coleridge, Lord Byron, Sir Walter Scott in England; Goethe, Heinrich Heine, in Germany; Victor Hugo in France; Pushkin and Gogol in Russia; and Mickiewicz in Poland. In music: von Weber, Schubert, Mendelssohn, Rossini, Bellini, Donizetti, and later Beethoven. In philosophy: Herder, Fichte, Hegel, possibly also Kant.

Most relevant to our topic is that the Romanticists glorified folk songs, native languages, and popular culture. They searched in people's histories for evidence of glorious actions. They called for a return to (the Rousseauvian) nature, and for an attention to the 'simple peasant', thus elevating the 'common man' to importance. The spirit of Romanticism became part of the nationalist spirit. Such a spirit could serve to unify radicals and liberals, middle class and peasants, rich and poor, nobility and clergy. The newly recognised, and apparently shared culture, history, folklore, *could* serve as foundations of a 'national' identity, around which a group of people form an 'us'.

Not all Romanticists were 'nationalists' and certainly few regarded themselves, or were regarded by others, as 'liberals'. On the other hand, probably most 'nationalists' were Romantic and many Romantics 'nationalists'. The Italian Giuseppe Mazzini (1805–72), for example, was such a Romantic nationalist leader. He was born in Genoa, jailed for secret society activities, exiled to Paris, organised Young Italy and set out to liberate Italy.

By 1830 the Metternich regime and the alliance he initiated in 1818 – the 'Concert of Europe' which consisted of the members of the Quadruple Alliance plus France – cracked. The 'practical solutions' of the Congress of Vienna of 1815 proved ineffective. As we shall see, they may even have contributed to the eventual eruption of the 1848 revolutions.

The Revolutions of 1848

The 1848 Revolutions – originating in France in 1847 – had little if anything to do with 'ethnic' or 'national' discontent initially. French students and workers demanded in demonstrations of February 1848 electoral reforms, universal suffrage, work for everyone. In March 1848 students and professionals in Vienna presented petitions for a new constitution, for universal franchise, a free press, jury trials, academic freedom, emancipation of peasants, and, repressed but not stopped, students demanded an end to religious discrimination. The civil guard refused to shoot. Possibly because Emperor Ferdinand I disapproved of sending the civil guard against students, he dismissed Metternich, who fled to England. In April 1848 a preliminary new constitution was proclaimed, but included far fewer rights than those demanded. In June and July 1848 the Constituent Assembly gathered to draft a permanent constitution for the Empire. At the same time, 24–26 June 1848, fighting erupted on the streets of Paris, but the forces of order prevailed.

The news of the 'February Revolution' also reached East-Central Europe, where it effected different types of demands, and the Revolutions of 1848 gained a different character.

Czechs in Bohemia asked for a constitutional government and equality with the German-speaking population in July 1848. It should be noted that the demand was not for sovereign independence but for autonomy within Austria-Hungary. The Czech historian and politician, Frantisek Palacky, and other Czech intellectuals, believed that the future of the Czechs was in a new, federated, Austro-Hungarian entity.

In Hungary, Kossuth demanded independence for Hungary; the Emperor, however, offered only autonomy. Accordingly, the Hungarian diet (parliament) passed the 'March Laws of 1848' which created a Hungarian constitutional monarchy *under* Habsburg rule. However, in April 1849 Kossuth, dissatisfied with such an arrangement, declared Hungary an independent republic. In reaction, Austrian, Russian and Croat troops invaded Hungary, defeating the

Hungarian forces. Austrian rule returned and Kossuth went into exile.

Slovenes, in the Austrian south-west, demanded ethnic (not territorial) autonomy within the six Austrian crownlands where they resided.

Then, there were demands posed to the Hungarian government by its own minorities. Serb demonstrators in the southern region of Hungary demanded autonomy, and were violently repressed by Hungarian troops in the spring of 1848. Transylvanian Romanians, opposing their incorporation into Hungary, first demanded a federal type of arrangement between Transylvania and Hungary; but in September 1848 they asked to be completely separated from Hungary in order to be attached to Austria, under its direct rule. Slovaks, in the north, agreed to autonomy within Hungary on condition that they receive linguistic and cultural autonomy, including education. Ruthenians in Galicia demanded autonomy in two regions within Galicia; Carpatho-Ruthenians in Hungary, in turn, demanded autonomy within Hungary. Both were refused. In addition to these demands, on 2 June 1848 a Pan Slavic Congress convened in Prague with the participation of Czech, Slovak, Yugo-slav, and Polish delegations and asked for 'liberty and autonomy' in the Habsburg Empire for the 'Slavic peoples'. That demand also fell on deaf ears.

The 1848 Revolutions failed to produce substantial 'national' victories. The Austro-Hungarian Empire survived virtually without changes until 1867. The question is: Why?

But, the more pertinent questions may be these: What caused the 1848 Revolutions in Central Europe and what accounts for their failure? What might account for the significance of these revolutions in retrospect, despite their failure to produce any meaningful victories? What might explain the survival of the Habsburg Empire for another two decades, to 1867, and in a new form to 1918?

H.G. Wells did not provide answers to these questions, but he did provide food for thought in the following passage:

> The 'nationality' which dominated the political thought of the nine-teenth century is really no more than the romantic and emotional exaggeration of the stresses produced by the discord of the natural political map with unsuitable political arrangements.[12]

According to another commentator, the explanation behind the failure of the Revolutions of 1848 was that no nationality had a majority. There were only 'dominant' and 'subordinate' minorities. The Empire was a mosaic of nationalities.[13] Pearson also noted that the real challenge to the Austrians of the Austro-Hungarian Empire came not from among the Magyar people but from the Hungarian nobility which composed some five per cent of the Hungarian population. Magyar nationalism was 'aristocratic in nature'.[14] The Hungarian nobility, large landowners, opposed not so much Austrian rule as the land reforms that the Austro-Hungarian central government promoted. They represented a class, rather than a nation. On the other hand, many among the Hungarian gentry traced their ancestry to the original Magyars, and had been regarded as such by the populations. These 'deep-rooted Magyars' – a rough translation of a well-known Hungarian phrase – were also less concerned with Austrian rule *per se* than with what they perceived to be a process of Germanisation resulting from Austrian domination.

The Hungarian intelligentsia, in turn, had absorbed French Revolutionary ideals and ideas of freedom and may be seen as romantic nationalists. Lastly, the Magyar 'nation' united against the cancellation in September 1848 of the autonomy attained in March 1848, and confronted the Austrians as one.

Had 'modernisation' in the Austro-Hungarian Empire enhanced Hungarian and other peoples' nationalism? Modern infrastructure – telegraph, roads – certainly quickened the *spread* of the ideas of the French Revolution. But the Hungarian nobility, which was exposed to these ideas, resisted Germanisation, the same as the nobility in the Balkans – which was far less exposed to it – resisted Ottomanisation. The conservative, landowning gentry resisted modernisation because it would have reduced their power.

We shall now look at the reorganisation of the Austro-Hungarian Empire prompted, in part, by the 1848 revolutions.

RESPONSE TO DIVERSITY AFTER 1867

The Hungarian national resolve intensified after the Hungarian Revolution of 1848. After 1848 Hungarian leaders could press their claims more successfully also. Several factors assisted them in this regard. These may include the Austrian repression in Hungary following the years 1848–49, the independence of Italy in 1860 which could have served as an example to follow, the Prussian armies' defeat of the Austrian armies in 1866 and the subsequent exclusion of Austria from the new North German Confederation – all of which weakened Austria's status and power. However, Hungarian success was only partial. The country did not gain independence. Instead, the Dual Monarchy was born through Ausgleich (Compromise) in 1867.[15]

The 'Compromise' was between long-standing Hungarian demands for total separation from Austria and various Austrian proposals. One unacceptable or unworkable Austrian proposal was that of the Austrian chancellor Belcredi in 1885, to create an Austrian federation (a so-called pentarchy) of five historic political entities: German-Alpine, Magyar-Hungarian, Bohemian-Moravian, Polish-Ruthenian, and Southern-Slav.

In the 1867 Compromise, the Austro-Hungarian Empire was divided into two entities, an Austrian (Cisleithania) and a Hungarian (Transleithania), while the crown, that is the monarch, and certain other institutions, remained common. More specifically, there was to be one ruler in the Dual Monarchy, the Emperor, who was to be called 'Emperor' in Austria and 'King' in Hungary. Thus, the two states, Austria and Hungary, formed a Dual Monarchy. Each monarchy was to have its own legislative body united under one ruler – the Emperor – and also share foreign affairs, and military and financial matters of concern to both partners. Expenditures were the joint decision of the two parliaments according to a fixed quota every ten years.[16] Thus, the Compromise of 1867 established the Austro-Hungarian Monarchy, in which Austria and Hungary were to be equal partners.

It seems useful to quote here at some length a clarification provided by Robert Kann:

> ... the Compromise was not an international treaty [between two sovereign states]. It was not a federation or confederation either. There was no state [nor government] above the two member states as in a federation, nor were they fully sovereign as in a confederation.

Neither were the Austrian and Hungarian versions of the Compromise embedded in the constitutional laws of both states completely alike. In other words, the Compromise represented a political structure *sui generis*.[17]

The Hungarians aimed at emphasising their independence; consequently, they did not want a joint parliament. However, there was a need to coordinate legislation. For that purpose, 20 representatives from each of the upper houses and 40 from each of the lower houses were to meet in rotation in Vienna and Budapest.

One example of needed coordination concerned 'minorities'. Hungarian leaders considered Hungary to be a Hungarian *national* state and set out on a road of Magyarisation of *minorities* in Hungary. From such a vantage point it was understandable that they did not wish that Austria continue the precedent-setting custom of providing autonomy to various *nationalities* within the Austrian part of the monarchy. Professing to be liberals and democrats nevertheless, the Hungarian leadership preferred representation of non-Magyars in the Hungarian parliament to the granting of autonomy to them. They preferred that Austrians have a similar arrangement for their *minorities*.

The challenges that the ethnic diversity posed to subsequent Hungarian governments appear to have been not only slightly more numerous than those confronting Austrian governments, but possibly more complex, hence more difficult to handle. Let us look at each separately.

Austria

In December 1867 the new Austrian parliament passed five constitutional laws, of which the second pertains to basic rights and national rights. Article 19, Statute 142 of the second law does not recognise ethnic groups as corporate bodies with the right of representation, but recognises the rights of individual citizens. It reads as follows:

> All ethnic groups [Volksstämme] in the state have equal rights and every ethnic group has the inviolable right to preserve and cultivate its nationality and language. The equality of all languages customary in

the crownlands [landesübliche Sprachen] are recognised in schools, government agencies, and public life.

In the lands inhabited by several ethnic groups, the public schools shall be organised in a way that every ethnic group receives the necessary funds for training in its own language without being compelled to learn the second language of any land.[18]

How did 'ethnic groups' perceive and react to this law, its implementation, and the Austrian governments' policies in general? The first answer to this question appears to be that, in most if not all cases, there were no 'ethnic group' reactions but various reactions *within* each group. The variety of reactions stemmed from the diverse political, ideological, and social positions of their holders. In other words Austria – like the Ottoman Empire – encompassed individuals with differing political interests, conservatives and liberals, landowners and peasants, and so on. Ethnic groups thus may be said to have lacked cohesiveness and unified goals.

Let us turn now to the various ethnic groups in Austria.

The Czechs. Their stand against Austrian rule was weak and splintered for several reasons. First, Czechs seem to have traditionally split in their loyalty. On the one hand, they were Slavs, and *as* Slavs they were 'pro-East' (Poland, Russia and Slovaks) at least in theory. On the other hand, many Czechs were heavily affected by Western ideas and Western European culture, hence were 'pro-West' in practice. (Prague, the capital, was after all one of the most culturally endowed cities in Europe.) Second, some three million German speakers resided in Czech lands, and they served as a considerable political force. Third, a politically significant difference could always emerge, for historical reasons, between Bohemians and Moravians. Lastly, the mere geographic location of Czech lands – north of, not east of, Austria (Prague itself is north-*west* of Vienna) and with correspondent means of land communication – additionally worked to reinforce German cultural and in general Western influence. Separation from Austria by no means obviously seemed advantageous to all Czechs. Provision of the law granting individual rights was adequate for many.

The Slovenes. Before the Revolution of 1848, the Slovenes in

Styria and Carniola, where they formed some 90 per cent of the population, were not very active politically. Because they shared the Roman Catholic religion of most Austrians, the Austrian government considered them as a cultural group. However, after the Revolution of 1848, there was Slovene participation in the Pan-Slav Congress in Prague, and liberal elements among Slovenes also tended toward some form of alliance with the Catholic and Slav Croats. This trend strengthened after the Compromise of 1867, but there was no apparent need for specific arrangements for Slovenes until the collapse of the Austrian-Hungarian monarchy in 1918.

Hungary

A Hungarian felt totally justified to be a nationalist in the face of Austrian rule, but did not understand why would 'minorities' under Hungarian rule be nationalists. During their revolution in March 1848 they were openly hostile toward Hungary's minorities, especially toward the Croats in the south and the Slovaks in the north. These minorities were considered not nationalists but traitors, because when Hungary was under Ottoman rule these minorities had risen against the Magyars and sided with the Ottomans. Nevertheless, the Magyar diet of the briefly autonomous Hungary did grant formal autonomy to minorities in July 1849. But Hungary lost its political status *vis-à-vis* Austria and the diet's legislation lost its legality.

The minority issue was picked up again in Hungary after the Compromise of 1867. One of the main architects of the new Hungarian Nationality Law (1868), (Statute XIV), was Joseph Eotvos, Hungarian intellectual, writer and Minister of Public Education. He believed that in order to solve 'nationality problems' a federation of all 'traditional historic entities' should be created and, within the federation, an ethnic administrative organisation on county and community levels.

However, this solution was unacceptable to others in the Hungarian government and was not incorporated in the Nationality Law. Hungary did not become a federation, and group rights were not recognised. Rights of individuals were guaranteed, in that the use of the various languages was allowed in church, in elementary and intermediary schools (but not in high schools and above), and in intercourse with government agencies.[19] In 1879, an electoral system was introduced in Hungary which assured Hungarian dominance in the parliament. Hungarians (about half of the population) had 405 seats. The other half of the population was represented thus: Romanians five, Slovaks three and, according to the Compromise of 1867, 40 Croats having the right to participate in debates concerning Croatia and Hungary.

This representation was obviously imbalanced, and may or may not have reflected the Hungarian attitude on the minority issue. Instead of engaging in an overall assessment, we shall quote here Robert Kann and then refer to minority cases separately.

> Magyar national policy [after the Anschluss] was free from racism in so far as it did not base the unequal treatment of minorities on ethnic ancestry but on the demand to give up national identification and accept unconditional conversion to Magyarism. Within these terms the system was willing to recognise equality of all Hungarian citizens, without further consideration of ethnic-racial origin.[20]

The Croats. The Croats were primarily under Hungarian control in the Austro-Hungarian Empire. To free themselves from that control Croat leaders did discuss in the early 1800s the possibility of forming a Southern Slav unity with Serbs and others (the Illyrian movement), but the efforts led nowhere.

In the 1848–49 Austrian repression of Magyar autonomy, the Croats fought against the Magyars. Nevertheless, in the 'Sylvester Patent of 1851', Croatia received independence from Hungary (but not from the Empire). After the Compromise this arrangement was changed to autonomy through a Hungarian-Croatian Compromise.

Like the Austrian-Hungarian Compromise, this Compromise was also a union between two states (the Hungarian and the Croat), except that this was a union between two unequals. Nonetheless, they too shared a ruler and some institutions in common. However, because of what has been noted as an unequal balance of power, the Croatian autonomy *vis-à-vis* Hungary was more restricted than that of Hungarian *vis-à-vis* Austria. The Croats were restricted to internal administration, education and judicial matters. The 'anointment' of a governor in Croatia, the *ban*, required the approval of the Hungarian parliament and he was often a Magyar. Also, 40 Croatian representatives in the Hungarian parliament represented Croatia only in matters common to the two states. In any event, the Croatian delegates could be easily outvoted by the Magyar majority.

Although this autonomy arrangement between Hungary and Croatia was restrictive, it proved more liberal than arrangements made by the Hungarian government with any other group in Hungary. No form of autonomy was granted to any other group. As might be extrapolated from this generalised reluctance, the Hungarian-Croat Compromise did not last long either. It was abolished in 1883, when Croats claimed Bosnia (freed from Ottoman rule) as part of their greater Croatia. Subsequently, the Hungarian government allied with the Serbs in Croatia in their quest to gain greater autonomy from the Croats.

Romanians in Transylvania. Transylvania became free from the Ottomans in 1691 and was under Austrian jurisdiction until 1848. During the 1848–49 war, Romanians supported the Austrians against the Hungarians and, as a reward, the Austrian crown recognised Romania as a 'nation'. Then the Romanians demanded to be part of a four-nation state but, their demand rejected, they were attached to Hungary without group rights.

Serbs. Partly Serb populated Vojvodina and the Banat – populated by Magyars as well – were incorporated into Hungary in 1860 and 1872 respectively. On the other hand, many Serbs lived in Croatia as a minority primarily in the Krajina region which, after the Compromise, had independent status. The Magyars supported these Serbs in their rivalry with the Croats, but this Serb-Croat rivalry was low-scale until the Serbs in Serbia gained independence from Turkey in 1878. After 1878 Serb national demands grew in all three regions – Vojvodina, Banat and Croatia.

Slovaks. The Slovaks were under Hungarian rule for centuries and their status after the Compromise did not change. Their intensive Magyarisation continued. What aggravated the situation of the Slovaks was that many of them were Lutherans, and that Church did not enjoy a special status. Furthermore, the Hungarian Catholics did not side with Catholic Slovaks. Nevertheless, it is interesting to note as a rather puzzling fact, that Slovak leaders demanded autonomy within Hungary rather than association with the Czechs, as did Father Andrej Hlinka, the godfather of the Slovak Peoples Party. It was only toward the end of World War I that Hlinka leaned toward the idea of union with the Czechs, which was, in turn, promoted by the Czech Tomas Masaryk.

*

In this chapter we aimed at providing a brief summary of some of the more salient attempts in the Austrian and Hungarian realm, if not always to 'solve' ethnic problems, at least attempts to respond peacefully to the challenge that they posed. In the Austro-Hungarian, as well as in the Ottoman, multiethnic Empires, centralisation, assimilation, Germanisation (or Ottomanisation), and modernisation countered the French Revolutionary ideals, which had implied autonomy, separation, decentralisation and which posed a perceived threat toward minorities from entrenched conservative elements.

The shake-up produced by the 1848 Revolutions failed, at least in part, because prior to the independence of neighbouring Germany and Italy, and prior to the creation of the Dual Monarchy, the alternative model to the then dominant Central European empire system was still hazy. This argument may seem to overlook the fact that Belgium and Greece, let alone Switzerland, all three gaining independence previously, could have served as such models. However, these precedents were less relevant to nationalists in Central Europe.

NOTES

1. S.A. Fisher, *The Middle East: A History*, 3rd edn (New York: Alfred A. Knopf, 1979), p. 207.
2. Kemal Karpat, 'The Ottoman Ethnic and Confessional Legacy in the Middle East', in Milton J. Esman and Itamar Rabinovich, eds, *Ethnicity, Pluralism and the State in the Middle East* (Ithaca: Cornell University Press, 1988), p. 45.
3. Fisher, op. cit., p. 315.
4. Ibid., p. 317.
5. Ibid., p. 319.
6. Karpat, op. cit., p. 35.
7. Ibid.
8. Ibid., p. 37.
9. Ibid.

10. Fisher, op. cit., p. 324.
11. H.G. Wells, *The Outline of History* (New York: Garden City Publishing Co. Inc., 1920), p. 960.
12. Ibid.
13. Raymond Pearson, *National Minorities in Eastern Europe, 1848–1945* (Macmillan Press, 1983), p.45 ff.
14. Ibid.
15. The official term, introduced in 1869, was Austro-Hungarian monarchy. But in later years, expressing Hungarian separatist tendencies, the term Austria-Hungary was used. This usage implied that there was no federal structure above the dual states. Cf. Robert Kann, *A History of the Habsburg Empire, 1526–1918* (University of California Press, 1974), p. 333.
16. For Hungarian versus other interpretations of the nature of the union see footnote 29 in Robert Kann, *The Multinational Empire*, 2 Vols (New York: Columbia University Press, 1950).
17. Kann, op. cit., p. 333.
18. Quoted in Kann, ibid., p. 339.
19. There was, however, another national law passed in specific regard to Croatians, the 1868 Hungarian-Croatian Law of Compromise (Statute XXX).
20. Kann, op. cit., p. 363.

3 Response to diversity – after World War I

The trigger of the war was the assassination of the Archduke Francis Ferdinand in Sarajevo, Bosnia's capital, on 28 June 1914. The Archduke was to be the next Emperor of Austria-Hungary; his assassins were Bosnian Serb members of the Black Hand, and they may have been trained and instructed in the Serbian capital of Belgrade. On 23 July a 48-hour ultimatum was submitted to the Serb government by Austria-Hungary. It included some seemingly acceptable demands, such as investigation of the crime, and some other, apparently unacceptable demands, such as that representatives of the Empire participate in the investigation. The Serb government, after consultation with Imperial Russia, rejected the ultimatum. In August, World War I broke out.

It was to be the war to end all wars. But this phrase referred to external wars, not to the threat of wars that 'minorities' might pose. Not that it could be out of mind. The ethnic problem or, as it was more often referred to at the time, the 'nationality problem', did not disappear during the war, nor did attempts to resolve it. At least one of the reasons for both the consistency of the problem and its attempted resolution was what Robert Kann refers to as the intensification of the 'radicalisation of the masses' during the war. According to Kann, this radicalisation was due, first of all, to the greater involvement of political émigrés in the affairs of their nationals and, second, to the deteriorating economic situation, food shortages and famine, among the peasants.[1]

One resolution, regarding the future of Austria, was proposed by Friedrich Neumann, a German pastor. His *Mitteleuropaprogramm*, a

plan for Mittel Europe (Central Europe), published in 1915, called
for an economic-, customs-, and military defence-union between
Germany and Austria, on the basis of a common language, culture
and nationality. Neumann's idea was in reality intended as a German-
Austrian reaction to the attempted breakaway of ethnic/national
groups from Austria. The *Mitteleuropaprogramm* may be seen as
the ideological foundation of a provisional national assembly for
Germany-Austria which gathered on 21 October 1918. Indeed, on
30 October 1918, a provisional German-Austrian Constitution was
proclaimed, and on 12 November 1918, a German-Austrian Republic.
Neither survived after the end of the war, which came a few weeks
later.

Some of the attempted breakaways from the Empire did succeed.
The Czechs Tomas Masaryk and Eduard Benes in exile were leading
figures of Czech nationalism since 1914, and it was from their exile that
they pressed foreign governments for independent Czech statehood.
The Czech parliamentarians in Austria, on the other hand – Czech
lands were still part of the Austrian section of the Dual Monarchy –
asked at the opening of the Austrian Parliament in May 1917 for the
conversion of Austria into a multinational federal state, which would
also include the Slovak territories then under Hungarian rule. This
proposal got nowhere. In June 1918, however, the French government recognised the Czech National Council in Paris as representing
the Czech nation which, for Benes and Masaryk, was a step in the
right direction. Subsequently, the American government recognised
the Czech nation's right to self-determination. Finally, Czech and
Slovak organisations in the United States, mobilised by the two
Czech leaders, signed, in Pittsburgh, the 'Pittsburgh Declaration',
calling for the independence of Czechoslovakia. The agreement
was that the Slovaks, still under nominal Hungarian rule, would
form an autonomous nation not in a federal Austria, as the Czech
parliamentarians proposed earlier, but in an independent Czecho-
slovak state. Of course, Slovak membership in Czechoslovakia
meant their secession from Hungary. Since the Hungarian government did not offer any alternative to the Slovaks – it did not have the
wherewithal to prevent the plan even if the Hungarian government
wished to do so – the secession transpired without official Hungarian
reaction.

The 'national question' in Hungary during the war was embedded in debates on the franchise between the political left and right. The conservative Prime Minister Tisza opposed the franchise and any liberal plans in regard to nationalities. Tisza, however, was forced to resign in May 1917 and was replaced, on 31 October, by Tisza's foremost liberal opponent, Count Mihály Karolyi, who, along with his supporters such as the historian-politician Oszkar Jaszi, was for national autonomy and general franchise, as well as breaking up the big estates. Tisza was assassinated the same day, probably by Red Guards, members of the radical left, who later took over the Hungarian government. As far as the Dual Monarchy was concerned, on 11 November 1918 Prime Minister Karolyi simply proclaimed Hungary a republic and thus severed ties with Austria.

In the southern part of the Austrian-Hungarian Dual Monarchy the idea of a 'Southern Slav Union' – existing as far back as the early years of the nineteenth century – was still alive. The union had its supporters and opponents, but, until the end of World War I, a Southern Slav union was intended by most of its supporters to be an autonomous entity within a wider framework, be it the Austrian or the Austro-Hungarian. As late as the opening of the Austrian parliamentary session in May 1917, Croat and Slovene representatives proposed a union of Southern Slavs *within* the monarchy. Nonetheless, the Corfu Declaration of 20 July 1917 proclaimed a union of Croats, Slovenes and Serbs as an independent state.

At least one aspect of the process that led to the independence of Yugo-slavia is important from the ethnic perspective. In the summer of 1918, National Councils were established in Carniola, Dalmatia, Bosnia and in Zagreb for Southern Slav peoples under Habsburg rule. Southern Slav peoples not under Austrian rule – Serbs, Macedonians, etc. – were excluded, for members of the new National Councils at first pursued the idea of federation within Habsburg Austria. By October 1918 they all agreed to separate from Austria and join with Serbia to form their own federal state.

Now, since Austria was defeated in the recently ended world war, so were those Southern Slavs who were part of the Austrian-Hungarian monarchy. Consequently, independent Serbia alone from among Southern Slavs was represented at the post-World War I Peace Conferences. The unintended results were that, first, the Serbian leadership obtained independence on their behalf for Southern Slavs (Yugoslavs). Second, since demarcating lines among the various Southern Slav peoples were blurred, internal boundaries among them could not be easily finalised within the newly established independent state. The later named Yugoslavia became independent on 1 December 1918 without an agreement on internal boundaries. They were to be finalised only during the creation of the post-World War II federation of Yugoslavia by President Tito, in 1946. In other words, the independent Southern Slav state emerged in 1918 as a potentially troublesome ethnic mosaic.

'SELF-DETERMINATION'

Plebiscites conducted in France after the French Revolution to find out whether or not the people of the papal enclaves – Avignon, Venaisssin, Savoy and Nice – wanted to be part of France, may have been one of the harbingers of the idea that citizens have a right to choose their rulers. However, not plebiscites proper but, conveying the same idea, self-determination, became the key concept during World War I, at the Peace Conferences that followed it, and in their aftermath, up to this day. Thus, not plebiscite, will of the people, but self-determination turned to be the indispensable central concept for discussion and assessment of the practical 'solutions' proposed to solve the 'minority problem' in Central Europe.

The apparently first explicit use of the phrase in a formal document was in the resolution of the 1896 International Socialist Congress in London, which stated that the Congress 'upholds the full rights of the self-determination of all *nations* ...' In 1903, still long before President Woodrow Wilson used the term, 'self-determination' was discussed at the Second Congress of the Russian Social-Democratic Labour Party. It proclaimed 'the right to self-determination for *all nations forming part of the state*'. Lenin too, in his 'Postulates on the National Question' restated, in 1913 – before the October Revolution of 1917 – 'the right of every nation to self-determination and even to secession from Russia'. In January 1915, already during the war, the Socialist Conference of Denmark, Holland, Norway and Sweden called for the 'recognition of the self-determination of nations'.[2] By the time Georges Clemenceau, Lloyd George and Woodrow Wilson referred to self-determination, the concept was widely known, frequently used in political debates and demands by various political actors, including leaders of national groups of Austria-Hungary and in the collapsing Ottoman Empire.

This brief history of the term may provide the impression that socialists (and communists) were the first to advocate self-determination. This is accurate to a degree. One might note, however, that many of the socialists and communists lived in countries plagued by ethnic and nationality problems of long standing. These individuals had long sought for ways to resolve the 'nationality problem' and self-determination appeared to them to be instrumental toward that goal. Thus, self-determination may be better seen not as part of the socialist doctrine, or an idea dictated by the Marxist ideology, but as a practical measure designed by political entrepreneurs and thinkers for the remedy of a concrete problem and, as such, preferable to other possible remedies, such as, on the one hand, tolerating it as a temporary phenomenon that will disappear either through modernisation or rising class consciousness or, on the other hand, allowing 'minorities' democratic representation.

In the United States, President Wilson was not confronted with the same kind of ethnic and nationality problems as were European intellectuals and statesmen. Also, his early political thinking was influenced by the ideals of the French and American Revolutions but, primarily, by the democratic ideal as practised in the United States. It is not surprising therefore that Wilson was a proponent not of self-determination of nations but of democratic rule of peoples. Wilson's political aim, as of American Presidents after him, was to strengthen and export democracy. In an address on 2 April 1917, some ten months before his Fourteen Points speech, Wilson said:

> A steadfast concert for peace can never be maintained except by a partnership of democratic nations. No autocratic government could be trusted to keep faith within it or observe its covenants ... The world must be made safe for democracy. Its peace must be planted upon the tested foundations of political liberty. We have no selfish ends to serve ... We are but one of the champions of the rights of mankind ...[3]

President Wilson was interested in spreading democracy. He adopted a phrase long used by European socialists, and joined the group of Allied statesmen in their commitment to self-determination during the war, in order to spread democracy.

The first pronouncement on self-determination on the side of Allied governments was probably made by the British Foreign Office, during the war, in January 1916. President Wilson merely reacted to it in the affirmative a few days later. Subsequent siding with the same principle were made by the governments of Italy, France, as well as that of Germany. In the following year, on 16 May 1917, Wilson still stated that '[n]o people must be forced under the sovereignty under which it does not wish to live',[4] which was no more than an expressed commitment to democracy. It was only on 8 January 1918, toward the end of the war, that Wilson announced his Fourteen Points to a joint session of Congress. Even then, Wilson's famous Fourteen Points declaration does not include the phrase 'self-determination'. Nonetheless, at least five of the points make allusions to it (see discussion further below). Also, in an address to Congress on 11 February 1918, the President did mention 'self-determination':

> National aspirations must be respected; peoples may now be domi-
> nated and governed only by their own consent. 'Self-determination' is
> not a mere phase [sic]. It is an imperative principle of action, which
> statesmen will henceforth ignore at their peril.[5]

Furthermore, although self-determination was not included in the Covenant of the League of Nations, which was President Wilson's brainchild, Wilson's first *draft* of the Covenant did contain the phrase 'principle of self-determination'. Ultimately, Wilson's Fourteen Points, together with his additional pronouncements on self-determination and their impact on the League of Nations, made Wilson the godfather of that moral principle.

Nevertheless, for Wilson, the phrase 'self-determination' became, and remained, the packaging outer-layer for democracy. An interesting question is why did Wilson package, or feel he had to package, democracy in the cloak of self-determination?

Wilson's Fourteen Points and his subsequent mentioning and

siding with the principle of self-determination occurred *after* the Bolshevik Revolution of October 1917. The pre-revolutionary Russian Provisional Government, echoing the declaration of the Socialist International, declared already in March 1917 that its war aim was peace on the basis of 'the right of nations to decide their own destinies'. Such a declaration was consistent with those made by Western powers at the time. However, on 15 November 1917, after the Bolshevik Revolution, the Soviets went further. They issued the Declaration of Rights of the Peoples of Russia. (There was no Soviet Union yet.) The Declaration also recognised the equality and sovereignty of Russia's nationalities, and the right of Russia's nationalities to *free self-determination* including *seceding* and organising an independent state. The same principles were included in the Soviet Constitution of 10 July 1918.

Furthermore, in December 1917 the Bolshevik government bid for peace which led to long negotiations between Russia and the Central powers (Germany and Austria-Hungary, as well as Bulgaria and Turkey) the enemies of the Allied powers. On 3 March 1918, the Treaty of Brest-Litovsk was signed between Russia and Germany. The significant point here is that the new Russian government did adhere to its own commitment to the principle of self-determination. It gave up large chunks of territories on Russia's western border where non-Russian peoples lived. In the Treaty of Brest-Litovsk, Russia – still during World War I – recognised the independence of Ukraine, Georgia and Finland; gave up Poland and the Baltic states; handed over parts of Byelorussia to Germany and Austria-Hungary; and ceded territories to Turkey. After Germany and Austria-Hungary lost the war, they had no choice but to renounce the Brest-Litovsk Treaty in the Armistice of 11 November 1918, and Russia, more specifically, the post-revolutionary government of the Soviet Union, also proclaimed it null and void. The western boundaries of the Soviet Union were settled after World War I by various treaties. For example, the boundary between Poland and the Soviet Union was fixed in the Treaty of Riga in 1921.

It seems that these series of acts by the Russian Bolshevik government were the ones that compelled Wilson – and other Western statesmen – to take the principle of self-determination seriously.

In keeping with the principle of democracy, President Wilson was clearly in favour of free choice for peoples under oppressive rule; and 'self-determination' was an acceptable, and in the given circumstances a useful, term for it. Points X, XI, and XII – the ones referring primarily to the region under the rule of the Austro-Hungarian Monarchy and the Ottoman Empire among his Fourteen Points – may serve as illustrations:

IX. The readjustment of the frontiers of Italy should be effected along clearly recognisable lines of nationality;

X. The peoples of Austria-Hungary, whose place among the nations we wish to see safeguarded and assured, should be accorded the freest opportunity of autonomous development;

XI. Rumania, Serbia, Montenegro should be evacuated; occupied territories restored; Serbia accorded free and secure access to the sea; and the relations of the several Balkan States to one another determined by friendly counsel along historically established lines of allegiance and nationality . . .;

XII. The Turkish portions of the present Ottoman Empire should be assured a secure sovereignty, but the other nationalities which are now under Turkish rule should be assured an undoubted security of life and an absolutely unmolested opportunity of autonomous development . . .;

The democratic component in Wilson's principle of self-determination may be seen in the fact that he did not advocate the 'dismemberment' of Austria-Hungary and granting self-determination to its 'peoples'; not in his Fourteen Points, nor late in 1918, months after his Fourteen Points. In his view – and that of the British and French governments – Austria-Hungary was an organisation of a variety of peoples, among them Czechs, Slovaks, Magyars, Croats and Slovenes. The dismemberment of Austria-Hungary would produce conflicts in the future. Wilson wanted to avoid another 'balkanisation' that is, what he viewed as the re-creation of the kind of ethnic mosaic that existed in the southern part of Europe, and which did produce conflicts before the war.

For Western statesmen it would have been politically impractical to oppose the principle of self-determination. Already during the war, and more forcefully towards its end, nationalist leaders of various 'subject peoples' of Austria-Hungary and the Ottoman

Empire – both later losers in the war – pressed for independence for the nations they purported to represent. In April 1918 a Congress of Oppressed Nationalities convened in Rome under Italian patronage with representations by Czechoslovaks, Rumanians, and South (Yugo) Slavs, who claimed the right to self-determination.

Wilson had little choice. He ultimately did consent to the dismemberment of Austria-Hungary. But, as he wished, dismemberment did not 'balkanise' the two Empires. Poland and a much truncated Hungary realised *national* self-determination. But, the dismemberment of Austria-Hungary and the Ottoman Empire also gave birth to the non-balkanised, multiethnic or multinational states of Czechoslovakia and Yugoslavia. Possibly as Wilson had wished, self-determination was granted not to ethnic groups or nations but to multiethnic or multinational states. In his eyes, it was for democracy to prevent the eruption of conflict within the sovereign ethnic mosaics.

The birth of the new states was legalised in international treaties. The most important one, the Treaty of Versailles of 28 June 1919, was one of five treaties signed at the end of World War I, and embodied the results of the Peace Conference negotiations. It was signed by the representatives of the United States, Britain, France, Italy, and by Germany, whose representatives did not participate in the negotiations. The Versailles Treaty included: (1) the establishment of the League of Nations; (2) creation of states according to the principles of national self-determination; (3) reparations to be paid by Germany; (4) the assigning of the region of Alsace-Lorraine to France; (5) putting German colonies under the mandate system; (6) giving Poznan and the Polish Corridor to Poland; and (7) arranging Danzig (Gdansk) to be a free city. The other post-World War I treaties were the Treaty of St Germain (relevant to Austria), the Treaty of Trianon (the 'dismemberment' of Hungary), of Neuilly (pertaining to Bulgaria), and of Sevres (relevant to Turkey).

THE PEACE CONFERENCES

By the time the post-World War I Peace Conference convened in 1919 all Western governments were committed to the principle of self-determination. However, the phrase was not included in the Covenant of the League of Nations; it had no legal status. Self-determination did become a moral principle and was referred to in the League's deliberations. The granting of independence to Czechoslovakia and Yugoslavia, for example, was anchored in the *moral* principle of self-determination, *not* in a *legal* obligation on the part of the international community.

Although the commitment to the moral principle of self-determination was deep and virtually universal, there were other considerations which limited its application. First, the victorious powers had no intention of applying the principle in their own countries; only in the defeated ones. Second, the principle was seen as relevant only to Europe, for 'whites only', and not to be extended to the dependent peoples in the colonies. Third, then, as in years to come, the major powers were primarily guided by what they perceived to be their national interests. Alfred Cobban, one of the prominent students of self-determination, observed:

> ... the British and American delegations [to the Paris Peace conference of 1919] were anxious to confine self-determination to Europe, while the French and Italian delegations would have preferred to confine it to Utopia.[6]

In addition to the fact that the principle of self-determination had limited applicability and often collided head-on with various national interests, it was also not always entirely clear how to ascertain the will of a population. The Germans, for example, demanded plebiscites in all but the areas to be ceded to Poland. Italians objected to plebiscites in regions not populated by Italians, and instead proposed peace negotiations about the modalities of relations among various nationalities. Americans, who had no particular national interest to promote in Central Europe at the time, preferred sending teams of experts, commissions, for the same purpose, rather than the holding of plebiscites.[7] The Romanians opposed the holding of plebiscites in Bessarabia which had only a Romanian minority, and the French preferred to claim Alsace-Lorraine from the Germans on historic grounds, rather than through a plebiscite. The Bolsheviks in Russia, in turn, favoured plebiscites in all territories they ceded to the

Germans in their treaty with them on 3 March 1918, at Brest-Litovsk. On the border region between Austria and Hungary a plebiscite was held in the city of Sopron which, abiding by the results, was awarded to Hungary.

In some other instances national leaders purported to represent the will of populations to members of the League. The Czechs, for example, had a prominent and highly effective leader in Jan Masaryk, who had a relatively easy task of arguing for the independence of Czechoslovakia. But Slovaks, Ruthens and others had no similarly effective leadership at the time. It was clear that Slovaks wanted to be free from Hungarian domination. If they had had an effective leadership they might have gained an independent Slovakia. Without such a leadership they had to compromise by becoming part of Czechoslovakia. Absence of effective leadership was probably one of the reasons for the birth of the multiethnic states of Czechoslovakia as well as Yugoslavia.

It was also suggested to the League by interested parties that those speaking the same language should be part of the same nation, and boundaries be adjusted accordingly. The Poles, for example, claimed territory from Germany on the basis of the language of the *inhabitants* that lived on it, which was Polish. But the Poles refused to abide by the same rule in the eastern borders with Russia, where Ukrainian, Russian and other Slavic languages were spoken, because the *territory* on which these people lived historically belonged to Poland. The Germans, on their part, did not accept the Polish claim on their eastern border, a traditionally German territory in their view, but claimed *language* as the basis everywhere else, including on their border with France.

Was the response of the Peace Conferences to the ethnic challenge in Central Europe satisfactory? It seems appropriate to say that it was not. The new map of post-World War I Central and Eastern Europe can hardly be seen to reflect the principle of self-determination. Self-determination was extended to *states*, not ethnic groups or nations, many of which resented their minority status. Czechoslovakia included Czechs, Slovaks, Ruthens and Germans; Hungary included Slovaks and Germans; Poland included Byelorussian and Ukrainian populations; Romania included Magyars, Germans and other non-Romanians; and Yugoslavia was to become a state of many 'peoples', ethnic groups or nations. Let us illustrate this argument with a concrete example.

Toward the end of World War I, in March 1918, the Bolshevik government of Russia surrendered to Germany territories in Ukraine and Byelorussia (White Russia) which were then occupied by German troops. These vast territories between Poland and Russia were called 'the Ober-Ost'. After the war ended, by the end of 1918, the German armies were evacuated from these territories and, on 14 February 1919, Russian forces from the East and Polish forces from the West entered the territory and clashed, in order to reclaim the parts their respective governments claimed before the war.[8] The Polish forces had the upper hand. On 25 April 1919 they had already marched on Kiev (capital of the Ukraine) – far beyond the Polish borders – which was defended by Russian forces.

Now, on 17 July 1920, the British Foreign Secretary, Lord Curzon, proposed in a telegram from London to Moscow an armistice line between the Polish and Russian forces, which became known as the Curzon Line. However, both the Polish and the Russian governments rejected the Curzon Line as a border between the two states and the war continued. It officially ended with the Peace Treaty of Riga on 18 March 1921. In the terms of that treaty the bulk of contested territories reverted to Poland, whereas, when the Poles entered the region on 14 February 1919, it was already inhabited by Lithuanians, Byelorussians and Ukrainians. Why this result? Probably because by 1921 the reduction of territories held by the Bolsheviks was more important to the West than the minority problem created by such a reduction.

On the eve of World War II, there was again a confrontation between Poland and the Soviet Union, which led to the infamous Hitler–Stalin Pact of 1939. In September 1939, before the Hitler–Stalin Pact, Soviet armies invaded the border areas in Poland which, according to the 1921 Peace Treaty of Riga, belonged to Poland. By that time these areas were already inhabited by some five million Poles through resettlement. Nevertheless, it was still inhabited also by about five million Ukrainians, and some 1.5 million Byelorussians.

Prior to that, a *temporary* peace had been restored after World War I, and the eruption of violent ethnic conflict was at least postponed. And, above all, self-determination had become part of the political vocabulary, and the League of Nations' concern with self-determination set a precedent; both factors obliged the founders of the United Nations to incorporate that principle in its Charter.

THE 'MINORITY PROBLEM' BETWEEN TWO WORLD WARS

The League of Nations did not fully implement the principle of self-determination; instead, it did make an effort at guaranteeing *minority rights*. The governments of newly recognised Poland, Romania, Czechoslovakia, Yugoslavia and Greece were forced to sign 'Minorities Treaties' with the 'Principal Allies and Associated Powers'. These treaties were to protect 'racial, religious, and linguistic minorities' from forced assimilation and discrimination and to guarantee them political rights, religious freedom, their own schools, and use of their languages. This was far short of self-determination. Alfred Cobban noted that the following ideas became a substitute for self-determination after the war:

a belief in small states as a justifiable part of the international order, a belief in the equality of states, great or small, and a belief in the right of absolute national sovereignty.[9]

The crucial point to realise is that guarantee of minority rights in post-World War I Europe did not solve what were labelled as 'minority problems'. Minorities were guaranteed civil rights, which was far short of their aspirations and, in some cases, their expectations. By safeguarding their civil rights but negating the right of minorities to self-determination, even autonomy status, let alone independence, the Commission of the League responsible for minorities in fact reinforced the rights of central *governments* to consolidate their states. Since most of the new governments were not democratic, and cared little about civil rights, 'minorities' lost on two accounts. Furthermore, the presence of dissatisfied minorities in multiethnic states provided the excuse and the opportunity for governments – purportedly concerned about the fate of their own nationals in neighbouring and not neighbouring states – to pursue their own national interests. Thus the Nazi German government's influence could grow among German minorities in the neighbouring states of Poland and Czechoslovakia largely because 'minority problems' were left unsolved there after World War I which, in turn, it seems safe to say, helped to pave the road to World War II.

Let us now look a bit more closely at the ways minorities fared in Central European states under consideration here.

Austria, totally separated from Hungary after World War I, was reorganised into eight *Länder*, each of which – plus a ninth, Vorarlberg – formed part of the federal Republic of Austria. (Vorarlberg, previously part of Tyrol and located next to Switzerland, was inhabited by a German-speaking population. A vast majority of its population voted in 1918 to become a canton in Switzerland, but after Austrian government objection, they became the inhabitants of an Austrian federal unit.) Burgenland in western Hungary, populated by German speakers, was also attached to Austria through a referendum. Slovenes in Carinthia voted to be part of Austria and were granted a degree of personal autonomy.[10]

Czechoslovakia. The Treaty of Trianon (1920) left some one million Hungarians within the Slovak inhabited regions of Czechoslovakia. This created a Hungarian 'minority problem'. However, the period from 1920 to 1939 was also studded with as many 'problems' between Czechs and Slovaks as between Slovaks and Magyars. The Slovak People's Party – whose first separatist foray from the Hungarian part of the Austrian-Hungarian Dual Monarchy under Father Andrej Hlinka had failed – was re-established in independent Czechoslovakia on 19 December 1918 under Father Josef Tiso, the successor to Hlinka, and pressed for the promised Slovak autonomy in Czechoslovakia. In 1927 a province of Moravia and Silesia was created in Czechoslovakia.

The changes that occurred on the eve of World War II are well-known historic facts. In the Munich Pact of 1938 the Sudetes, Silesia, North-West and Southern Moravia were incorporated into Germany; Slovakia first became an autonomous state within Czech-Slovakia; then, in 1939, Moravia and Bohemia became German protectorates, and Slovakia a nominally independent republic under German protection.

Yugoslavia. Since we shall focus on Yugoslavia in a separate chapter, only a few salient post-World War I events will be mentioned here.

Perhaps first in importance is the Croat nationalists' pressing for complete independence from Yugoslavia, which was supported in the 1930s by the Italian fascist leader Mussolini. Possibly in attempted response, Croatia – comprising also Dalmatia on the Adriatic Sea and parts of Bosnia-Herzegovina – was allowed by the government in Belgrade to form an autonomous *banovina* (Ban is the equivalent title of viceroy) in 1939. However, the primarily Croat fascist organisation, Ustashi, continued to pursue the issue of independence, so that when Nazi Germany invaded Yugoslavia in 1941 during World War II, the Ustashi declared the independence of Croatia under the fascist leader Ante Pavelic.

Also in the 1930s, an Internal Macedonian Revolutionary Organisation (IMRO) – probably supported by the Bulgarian government – agitated against Serbian rule in Macedonia. In 1934 a Macedonian assassinated King Alexander of Yugoslavia.

After the Treaty of Trianon the German-speaking minority in Backa became citizens of Yugoslavia. According to a 1910 census there were 301,000 German-speakers in Vojvodina alone, alongside 421,500 Magyars and 381,000 Serbs.

With Hitler's rise to power in Germany, German identity in the Backa gained strength, which eased Hungarian occupation of Backa in the early years of World War II. In 1944, with the advance of Tito's partisans and Russian armies, some of the Germans of Backa fled, others stayed. An estimated 150,000 of the Germans of Vojvodina were imprisoned or executed as war criminals, and about 450,000 were deported.[11]

The Banat, most of it forming part of Hungary initially, was promised by the Allies during World War I to be attached to Romania. However, in the Treaty of Trianon, 1920, Banat was divided. The northern part, inhabited mainly by Magyars, was attached to Hungary, the eastern – mainly Romanian – part went to Romania, and the rest of Banat to Serbia.

Transylvania, inhabited by Hungarians and Romanians, had a checkered history. It was freed from the Ottomans by Austro-Hungarian armies in 1691 and fell under Austrian jurisdiction until

1848. That year Transylvania was (re)attached to Hungary. In response, Romanians supported the Austrians in the Hungarian war of 1848 against the Austrians. As a reward, the Austrian crown recognised Romanians in Transylvania as a 'nation'. However, in the Compromise of 1867 Transylvania was handed back to Hungary.

During World War II, on 1 July 1940, the Hungarian Nazi Party accused the Romanian government of evicting Hungarians from Transylvania in order to make room for Romanian refugees transferred from Bessarabia, which was then attached to the Soviet Union. Although the Romanian government offered an exchange of population to the Hungarian government, and some territorial concessions, its offers were rejected. Negotiations between the two governments continued on 16 and 24 August 1940, but eventually they broke off. Finally, on 30 August 1940, Hitler imposed boundary changes, the 'Viennese arbitration', in favour of Hungary. To reciprocate for Hitler's intervention, the Hungarian government accorded privileged status to Germans in Hungary.

*

The 'minority problem' was not exclusive to the new states emerging from defeated Austria-Hungary and the Ottoman Empire. There were 'minority problems' between the two world wars in the British Empire (Egypt, India, Iraq) and in the French Empire (in the Middle East and Africa). There were also 'nationalist' insurrections in Wales and Scotland; in Brittany and Flanders on the western coast of Europe; and in Alsace, between France and Germany. In Spain, Catalans and Basques rebelled. The problem had become widespread and post-World War I measures could hardly serve as a model for their solutions.

NOTES

1. R. Kann, *A History of the Habsburg Empire, 1526–1918* (University of California Press, 1974) p. 497 ff.
2. Dov Ronen, *The Quest for Self-Determination* (New Haven: Yale University Press, 1979), especially Chapter 2.
3. Herbert Hoover, *The Ordeal of Woodrow Wilson* (New York: McGraw-Hill, 1958) pp. 18–19.
4. Quoted in D. Ronen, op. cit., p. 31.

5. Quoted in Hoover, op. cit., p. 23.
6. A. Cobban, *The Nation-State and National Self-Determination* (New York: Thomas E. Crowell, 1969) p. 66.
7. The United States government prevailed at times. For example, to ascertain wishes of populations in Transylvania, claimed by both Hungary and Romania, a fact-finding commission was sent there.
8. The territories the Polish government claimed were Polish territories before the partitioning of Poland by Russia, Prussia, and Austria in 1772, 1793, and 1795.
9. Cobban, op. cit., p. 75.
10. Fried Esterbauer, 'Austrian Experiences in Utilising Federalism to Conciliate Ethnic Minorities', in Daniel J. Elazar, ed., *Federalism and Political Integration* (New York: The University Press of America, 1984) p. 145.
11. Stephen Borsody, ed., *The Hungarians: A Divided Nation* (New Haven: Yale Center for International and Area Studies, 1988) p. 191.

4 Response to diversity – after World War II

In the midst of World War II the United States President Franklin D. Roosevelt and the British Prime Minister Winston Churchill met on a ship on the Atlantic Ocean in August 1941 and signed the 'Atlantic Charter' for a peaceful world. In Articles 2 and 3 of the Atlantic Charter Roosevelt and Churchill made a commitment to the principle of self-determination. In Article 2 they expressed the 'desire to see no territorial changes that do not accord with the freely expressed wishes of the people concerned'; in Article 3 they committed to

> respect the right of all peoples to choose the form of government under which they wish to live; and they wish to see sovereign rights and self-government restored to those who have been forcibly deprived of them ... [1]

In a memorandum written a few days after the signing of the Atlantic Charter, Roosevelt mentioned the term self-determination in a telling fashion, and referred specifically to the Croats:

> The self-determination of boundaries and forms of governments was the most substantial contribution made by the Versailles Treaty – i.e., the plebiscite method, which, on the whole was successful. This method can be extended in the case of certain populations and areas which have conducted century-old feuds. As an example, the people of Croatia should not be forced into a government with the Serbs, or with the Italians, or with the Hungarians, or compulsory independence by themselves, without an expression of their own views. [2]

When the two statesmen met with Stalin in 1943 in Iran at the

Teheran Conference, the victory of the three Allies was not in doubt. By the time the Yalta Conference among the three convened in Crimea on 4 February 1945, the Soviet forces had totally liberated their own country and swept through the Baltic states, eastern and western Poland, most of Hungary (including Budapest), all the Slovak part and much of the Czech part of Czechoslovakia, and were approaching the Oder River line in Germany. Romania, Finland, and Bulgaria – earlier occupied by and thus participating on the German side – capitulated to the advancing Soviet forces. By that time, American and British forces had already landed in Normandy on the western front, setting out to liberate France and Belgium, and penetrating the Rhineland on the western borders of Germany.

The next Allied conference was held just a few miles from occupied Berlin, at Potsdam, a few months after Yalta, from 17 July to 2 August 1945. The Potsdam Conference of the three victorious Powers was convened to confirm the agreements of Yalta, including the administrative division of Germany into four zones, and the transfer of all powers in Germany to the military commanders of the United States, the USSR, Great Britain, and France.

Still another event should be mentioned as background – the signing of the Charter of the United Nations by delegates of 51 states on 26 June 1945. It is noteworthy, that the signing of the Charter occurred before the end of World War II in August 1945, before the 'outbreak' of the Cold War, and before the start of the long process of decolonisation. In its Charter, the United Nations was committed to advance world peace, promote human rights and social and economic progress. It also included a commitment to the promotion of self-government for people in 'non-self-governing territories'. It did not apply to territories inhabited by 'minorities' in Central Europe.

The phrase 'self-determination' also appeared in the Charter of the United Nations: it did not apply to Central European minorities either. The phrase did appear twice: in Chapter I, Article 1, which lists the 'Purposes of the United Nations', Paragraph 2 includes among the Purposes:

> To develop friendly relations among nations based on respect for the principle of equal rights and self-determination of peoples, and to take other appropriate measures to strengthen universal peace.

In Chapter IX, devoted to 'International Economic and Social Cooperation', Article 55 mentions 'respect for equal rights and self-determination of peoples'.

In addition to these two specific mentions of 'self-determination' there were also two phrases in Chapters XI and XII of the Charter which today connote self-determination. One was 'self-government', the other 'independence'.

These were then the initial post-World War II policy statements and legal references to self-determination and to the ways of resolving minority problems around the world. With the passage of time policies changed and additional legal references were made.

PRIOR TO THE COLD WAR, 1945–48

The pronouncements made in the Atlantic Charter and the Charter of the United Nations raised hopes that the 'injustices' committed against minorities in post-World War I settlements could be rectified after World War II. Diplomatic activities carried out during the war seemed encouraging.

The Hungarian government, in secret negotiations with the Allies in 1943, prior to German occupation of the country in March 1944, prepared a proposal, which included a Danubian cooperation or federation. Churchill was in favour of a confederation and proposed it to the Soviet Foreign Minister Molotov in October 1943. Molotov rejected it.[3]

In a note to the Allies on Hungary's peace aims, dated 14 August 1945, a Danubian economic cooperation was again suggested. This time, the reference to 'nationalities' was spelled out. The note said among others:

> The most effective measure to counteract national antagonism ... would be the delimitation of boundaries according to the freely expressed will of the population and to the principles of nationality wherever the nationalities lie on contiguous territories.[4]

The Hungarian government also proposed transfer of populations in certain cases, and extending international protection of minorities in others. The immediate post-World War II Hungarian leadership hoped that although Hungary was again on the losing side in a war, the injustices of the Treaty of Trianon could be rectified. All these were vain efforts. Magyar minorities were included in neighbouring countries – in the Slovak part of Czechoslovakia, in Vojvodina and Backa in Yugoslavia, and in the Transylvania region of Romania. Since Hungary fought alongside the Germans to the end of the war – while Czechs and Yugoslavs fought on the side of the Allies and the Romanian government switched over from the German side to the side of the Allies – Hungarian proposals had little chance of being accepted. A federal arrangement was not to be and Hungary had to return to the borders of 31 December 1937.[5]

The following are among the changes which occurred in the immediate post-World War II period:

Magyars and Germans in Czechoslovakia

One of the more complicated minority issues in East Central Europe was that of Magyars in neighbouring countries. Hungarian-speaking minorities in Slovakia was one of these issues.

Slovakia was under Hungarian rule for centuries. When Czechoslovakia became independent in 1918, the borders were drawn so that some 600,000 Hungarian speakers were included within them. The Munich appeasement of 1938 – diplomatic moves by the West to satisfy some of the wishes of Hitler, restrain him and thus prevent the outbreak of war – included the transfer from Czechoslovakia to Hungary of some Hungarian and other mixed population territories. This act was referred to as the Vienna Award. After the war, in 1945, at the peace conferences, the Hungarian government demanded the return of Magyar population in Slovakia with the land on which they lived. In other words, Hungarians demanded population and territory, claiming that they had been under Hungarian rule for hundreds of years. Their demand was denied and what Hungarians considered 'lost territories' – along with some 600,000 Magyars living on them – were restored to Czechoslovakia.[6]

An added complexity was that the same Benes who during World War I was instrumental, along with Masaryk, in obtaining independence for Czechoslovakia in 1918 and after World War II became its president, obtained from the Allies, during the war, the formal recognition of Czechoslovakia's legal continuity. This meant that both Nazi occupied Czechs and Nazi collaborator Slovaks were considered citizens of a liberated Czechoslovakia. Hungarian and German minorities in post-World War II Czechoslovakia, by contrast, were seen by Benes as traitors who contributed to the break-up of Czechoslovakia.

The Benes government's 'Kosice Program' of 5 April 1945 – named after a town in Slovakia – provided for the confiscation of property of Germans and Hungarians who had 'actively helped' the Nazi enemy. A 22 June 1945 decree provided for the confiscation of property of *all* Germans and Hungarians in Czechoslovakia, and on 2 August 1945, a presidential decree deprived Czechoslovak citizenship from Germans and Magyars who could not prove to have assisted the Allies during the war. Subsequently, Hungarians were transferred either to Hungary or to Sudetenland, areas from which Germans were expelled.

Ultimately, an exchange of population was agreed upon between Hungary and Czechoslovakia on 27 February 1946, as a result of which up to 100,000 Slovaks could choose to transfer to Czechoslovakia and the same number of Magyars could choose to transfer to Hungary.[7] Eventually, some 60,000 persons were exchanged on each side.

Magyars in Transylvania

Both the Hungarian and Romanian governments posted claims to Transylvania during the war. Both were rebuffed.

Then, on 23 August 1944 the Romanian government switched to the Allies' side, and in the autumn of the same year Transylvania was occupied by Romanian and Allied Soviet forces. When Romanian forces carried out brutal reprisals against Magyars in November, the Soviets placed Transylvania under direct Soviet military administration. A new Romanian government was appointed in March 1945, and on 9 March Stalin agreed to the retransfer of Transylvania to Romanian administration on the condition that equal rights of minorities be guaranteed.

Needless to say, the Hungarian government protested the transfer of Transylvania. A Hungarian delegation went to Moscow in April 1945 with two alternative proposals. One proposal was to transfer

22,000 square kilometres of Transylvania to Hungary. Although such a large area had a Romanian majority population, it was comparable in size to the number of Magyars who would have remained in Romania proper, thus equal treatment of the respective minorities could be assured. The other proposal was to transfer only 11,000 square kilometres which had a majority of Hungarian inhabitants. The Soviet government refused to negotiate with the Hungarian delegation and advised it to negotiate directly with the Romanian government, which the Romanian government refused.

While the Hungarian Prime Minister Imre Nagy was in Washington in May 1946, pleading for American support of the Hungarian claims, the transfer of Transylvania to Romania was agreed to by all the Allies. This meant the reconfirmation of the Trianon settlement (1920). As of 1994, the status of Transylvania, and the Hungarian dissatisfaction with the arrangement, have not changed.

Hungary and Yugoslavia

Some 500,000 Magyars lived in Yugoslavia, most of them in Vojvodina which in 1945 was made an autonomous region in the Serbian Republic of Yugoslavia. In September 1946 a bilateral agreement provided for a voluntary exchange of up to 40,000 Magyars and Yugoslavs. It was never implemented.

Ruthenians in Czechoslovakia

Ruthenia, renamed Carpato-Ukraine, had a Ukrainian majority and, among other minorities, 150,000 Magyars. President Benes of Czechoslovakia ceded the region to the Soviet Union in an agreement signed on 19 June 1945.

DURING THE COLD WAR, 1948–89

From the end of World War II in 1945 to 1948, for roughly three years, the United States, Great Britain, France and the Soviet Union remained Allies and dealt with various post-war problems in Central Europe mostly through diplomatic channels. The political situation changed in 1948. Central European states – except for Yugoslavia which broke away from Moscow – fell into the Soviet camp. The record seems to show that from then on, policies – though not necessarily all actions – of communist governments toward the 'nationality problem' had changed for the better.

For example, a Hungarian scholar noted that after the communist takeover in February 1948, 'Slovakia's Hungarians slowly recovered from the blows of the rule of terror'[8] and that Hungarian language schools gradually opened. About 90 per cent of Magyar-speaking children in Czechoslovakia attended primary schools in their mother tongue within a few years.[9] The 1960 Constitution guaranteed 'equal rights of all citizens irrespective of nationality or race' and the right of 'citizens of Hungarian, Ukrainian, and Polish nationality to education in their mother tongues and all possibilities and means of their cultural development'. However, the conditions of Hungarians deteriorated considerably after 1968.[10] The 1968 Constitution re-asserted Czechoslovakia as a federation of Czechs and Slovaks. The Slovak partner of the federation had its own parliament and administration, and the Magyars fell, constitutionally, under direct Slovak rule. Demands of autonomy for Magyars continued to be presented, but in the new federal arrangement had no chance of being granted.

The communist regimes in Central Europe did not 'solve' the 'nationality problem'. Nevertheless, two observations relevant to that problem seem appropriate. First, it is probably safe to say that relative tranquillity in the sphere of ethnic and national conflict was greater and longer lasting in Central Europe during the Cold War years, 1948–89, than at any time since the French Revolution. Surely, it may be explained by the repression by the respective communist governments. However, that brings us to the second point in the form of a few questions. Did Western governments consider the above-mentioned repression important enough to put the 'nationality question' at the top of their policy agenda? Did Western governments advocate self-determination of 'minorities', or 'nationalities', behind the now fallen Iron Curtain, either on legal or moral bases during the Cold War?

Western governments' publicly stated foreign policies seem to show that encouragement of the struggle for self-determination by the various 'minorities' was not their priority. Instead, priority was given to nuclear and strategic considerations, limitation of the Soviet government's foreign influence, democratisation of regimes and other issues emerging from time to time, all within the framework of super-power confrontation. The issue of self-determination of peoples, that is, the inhabitants of states under communist rule, was forcefully promoted mainly by exiled groups in the West, by Voice of America broadcasts and by other governmental public and private efforts.

All in all, Western governments primarily supported and aimed to export democracy, as Woodrow Wilson had decades earlier. There was, however, a difference. Unlike President Wilson, Western statesmen during the Cold War did not hide democracy behind the noble slogan of self-determination. Just the opposite. Strategic, political, and economic aims were hidden under the noble slogan of democracy. This may explain, at least in part, the surprise that the re-emergence of the self-determination issue generated after the end of the Cold War.

But, how to interpret the fact that the United Nations did enact the 'International Covenants on Human Rights' in 1966? The fact is that both the 'International Covenant of Economic, Social and Cultural Rights' and the 'International Covenant on Civil and Political Rights' contain in their Article 1 the same statement:

> All peoples have the right to self-determination. By virtue of that right they freely determine their political status and freely pursue their economic, social and cultural development.

An explanation for such United Nations declarations and for Western governments' concomitant minimalisation of concern with 'minorities' or 'nationalities' is not difficult to come by.

During decolonisation, 'peoples' inhabiting colonies had exercised the right of self-determination by becoming citizens of independent states within inherited boundaries. 'Minorities' or 'nationalities' within these states had no right to self-determination. In fact the phrases 'nationalities' and 'minorities' virtually disappeared from the vocabulary. In the precedent setting process of decolonisation, the right to self-determination was accorded to 'people' defined by existing boundaries. Not surprisingly, 'peoples' residing within existing boundaries were encouraged to exercise their right to self-determination under communist rule as well. In other words, since formerly colonised peoples inherited the colonial boundaries, whatever might be their ethnic or 'nationality' composition, self-determination has been applied to 'peoples' in existing states everywhere. That type of self-determination was referred to in the United Nations' Covenants as well. 'Nationalities' did not fit the category of 'peoples'.

Let us recall, minority rights were of concern to the League of Nations. After World War I the notion of 'extraterritorial autonomy' – advocated by the Austrian socialists since the end of the nineteenth century and during World War I – was still prevalent.[11] Accordingly, the five newly created or recreated states – Czechoslovakia, Poland, Romania, Greece and Yugoslavia – were 'required' to sign Minority Treaties with the Principal Allied and Associated Powers.[12] In addition, there was a Minority Protection System 'to guarantee to some national minorities a measure of autonomy within the new states'.[13]

Such concern had largely disappeared during the Cold War. The United Nations had come to be preoccupied with decolonisation, and its agenda and vocabulary permeated all other issues. The switch of concern from the World War I period to the post-World War II period is well illuminated by a prominent student of self-determination, W. Ofuatey-Kodjoe:

> The way in which international society responds to such principles as self-determination is conditioned in an important way by who is making the claim. It will be recalled that in the final stages of World War I the groups that were agitating for self-determination and independence were the European nationalities. They were making the claims. Therefore, the question of self-determination was posed as 'national self-determination'. .... After World War II, it was not the European nationalities in revolt, it was overseas colonies. It was they who were making the claim. Thus, the answers have been provided in relation to colonial peoples – self-determination of peoples.[14]

The same concern was later transposed from colonial peoples to peoples under communist rule. Thus, during the Hungarian crisis of 1956, for example, the United Nations General Assembly adopted Resolutions 1004 (ES-II) and 1005 (ES-II), 'upholding the right of the Hungarian people to self-determination and calling on the Soviet Union to take steps to respect that right'.[15]

Policy support for 'peoples' right to self-determination – that is, the right of the inhabitants of sovereign states to self-determination, not of 'minorities' – also implied foreign policy support for the principle of non-intervention in the internal affairs of states, the territorial integrity of states, and the concomitant non-violability of their borders.

During the Cold War era, the rights of 'nationalities', or 'minorities', were not a major concern of Western governments or international organisations. Interest in these issues emerged in the late 1980s and became urgent only when the crises erupted in the former Yugoslavia, which may be dated to January 1992. We shall illustrate this argument by the following example.

The famous Helsinki Final Act (1975) of the Conference on Security and Co-operation in Europe (CSCE)[16] – which did become an important reference point for democratic forces in later years – was concluded a decade before President Gorbachev came to power in the Soviet Union, and long before the collapse of the Soviet Union and Yugoslavia. Among the 35 signatories of the Final Act were Bulgaria, Czechoslovakia, German Democratic Republic, Hungary, Poland, Romania, Yugoslavia, Canada, the Soviet Union and the United States.

One of the concerns of the Helsinki Final Act was 'Principles Guiding Relations Between Participating States'. It expressed respect for 'the right of every *State* ... to territorial integrity and to ... political independence.'

Another concern of the Helsinki Final Act was the *inviolability of frontiers*. It says that '[t]he participating States will refrain from any action ... against the territorial integrity, political independence, or the unity of any participating State ...' It adds that such states will also 'refrain from any *intervention*, direct or indirect ... in the internal and external affairs falling within the domestic jurisdiction of another participating State ...'

There was also a statement about human rights. The Helsinki Final Act stated:

> The participating States will respect human rights and fundamental freedoms ... without distinction as to race, sex, language or religion; ... will promote and encourage the effective exercise of civil, political,

economic, social, cultural and other rights and freedoms; ... recognise
and respect religious freedom; and recognise the universal significance
of human rights and fundamental freedoms ...

However, the reference here was not to the rights of 'minorities'.
The Helsinki Final Act did not refer to group rights, but to the rights
of 'persons'. Thus: 'The participating States on whose territory
national minorities exist will *respect the right of persons* belonging to
such minorities to equality before the law ...'

In connection with self-determination it said that '[t]he participating States will respect the equal rights of *peoples* and their right
to self-determination, acting at all times in conformity with the
purposes and principles of the Charter of the United Nations and
with the relevant norms of international law, *including those relating to
territorial integrity of States*. In other words, the right of 'peoples' to
self-determination does *not* entail a right of secession.

In order to be very clear on this point it was added that '[b]y virtue
of the principle of equal rights and self-determination of peoples, all
peoples always have the right ... to determine ... their internal and
external political status ...' and '... respect for and effective exercise
of equal rights and self-determination of peoples for the development
of friendly relations among themselves as among all states ...'

Until the eruption of ethnic conflicts in Yugoslavia, minority
rights were of little concern to Western governments in general and
the United Nations in particular.[17]

IN THE POST-COLD WAR ERA

With the end of the Cold War, which we date to the tearing down of
the Berlin Wall in November 1989, first the Baltic states – the Union
Republics of Estonia, Latvia and Lithuania – broke away from the
Soviet Union. The other Union republics followed later. The peaceful
division of Czechoslovakia into Czech and Slovak republics came on
1 January 1993. In the meantime, negotiations for reforming the
Yugoslav federation failed and collapsed through violent ethnic
conflict.

Apart from these well-publicised secessionist cases, several 'minority problems' continued brewing – in Slovakia, Transylvania, Vojvodina – and, outside of Central Europe, in Azerbidjan, Georgia and elsewhere in the former Soviet Union. By the early 1990s, prospects for the spread and intensification of ethnic conflict and extreme nationalist manifestations in Central Europe appeared serious.

The question that interests us here is this: What kind of policies, or practical solutions have been proposed and undertaken in response to the apparent 'ethnic challenge' in the post-Cold War era?

It seems clear that the 'minority problem' failed to gain priority until the eruption of ethnic conflict in Yugoslavia. The transition was not easy from a Cold War foreign policy concern with 'modern' super-power confrontation to a concern with what has been perceived as 'pre-modern' ethnic quarrels. Indeed, the transition was relatively slow. We shall again look at major international documents to prove our point.

The Charter of Paris for a New Europe[18] was signed and published on 21 November 1990, *after* the crumbling of the Berlin Wall, but before the outbreak of large-scale violence in Yugoslavia. A transition indeed occurred. While the Helsinki Final Act concentrated on territorial integrity and relations among states, The Charter of Paris shifted the focus to democracy and elections, i.e., democratisation. The issue of human rights also appeared, and that in the new context of democratisation, in the context of transition from repressive rule to democracy. The Charter stated:

> We undertake to build, consolidate and strengthen democracy as the only system of government of our nations. In this endeavour, we will abide by the following:
> - 'Human rights and fundamental freedoms ...' the protection of which is 'the first responsibility of government' ... and 'an essential safeguard against an over-mighty State.'
> - 'Democracy is the best safeguard of freedom of expression, tolerance of all groups of society, and equality of opportunity for each person.' [Note the *democratic* right of 'opportunity'.]
> - 'We affirm that, without discrimination, every *individual* has the right' to various freedoms, including the right 'to own property alone or in association and to exercise individual enterprise, to enjoy his economic, social and cultural rights'.

Minority issues were also discussed at various conferences of the CSCE, including the follow up meetings to the Madrid Conference (1980–83), the Copenhagen Meeting of the Conference on the Human Dimension of the CSCE States' Foreign Ministers in June 1990, Ottawa (1985) and Paris (1989). But, the Conference of Copenhagen that convened in 1989 and produced the 'Copenhagen Document', merely expressed the conviction that pluralistic democracy and the rule of law are essential for ensuring respect for all human rights and fundamental freedoms.

It was the Report of the Expert Meeting on National Minorities (Geneva, 1991) which laid down a 'shopping list' of approaches to the minority problem. It declared that 'different methods are suitable in the case of the implementation of the CSCE commitments concerning national minorities'.

At the time of the signing of the Charter of Paris, in November 1990, prior to the eruption of conflict in Yugoslavia, there was no significant change of tone from the declaration of the Helsinki Final Act in regard to minorities. It merely said:

> [w]e affirm that the ethnic, cultural, linguistic and religious identity of national minorities will be protected and that *persons* belonging to national minorities have the right to freely express, preserve and develop that identity ...

The CSCE also offered general principles concerning the Human Dimension (the Copenhagen Meeting of the Conference on the Human Dimension of the CSCE States' Foreign Ministers in June 1990), including national minority issues and ways to implement minority rights on national and international levels. Within the framework of the 'Human Dimension Mechanism', finding and implementing solutions is in the hands of the Office for Democratic Institutions and Human Rights (ODIHR) in Warsaw. The mechanism of 'Human Dimension' may only be activated by CSCE *participating states or by a state directly concerned*. Individuals cannot apply, but individual cases may be recognised through a legal procedure.

As of this writing the 'Human Dimension' mechanism has been activated three times: *vis-à-vis* Croatia and Bosnia-Herzegovina concerning attacks on unarmed civilians; in Estonia, in the case of legislative matters concerning human rights; and in Moldava. To what extent the 'Human Dimension' can be activated in future cases remains to be seen.

The focus of the 'international community' shifted again by the summer of 1991, *after* the governments of Croatia and Slovenia declared independence (on 29 May and 25 June respectively). At a meeting in Brussels on 27 August 1991 an 'Arbitration Commission' was set up by the European Community composed of five members chosen from the Presidents of Constitutional Courts in European Community member states. The Arbitration Commission was to 'enhance the rule of law in the settlement of the differences relating to the Yugoslav crisis'.[19]

Finally, the Helsinki Document of July 1992 was produced at a meeting of heads of states and government. One of the results of this meeting was the appointment of a High Commissioner of National Minorities (HCNM) in November 1992. The first HCNM, former Foreign Minister of the Netherlands, Max van der Stoel, took office in January 1993. His mandate was to prevent conflicts, and for this purpose he was to provide 'early warning' and, as appropriate, 'early action' in regard to tensions involving national minority issues. There was also a proposition to appoint sub-regional and national Ombudsmen for minorities.

*

We have started our narrative on the post-World War II era with a reference to self-determination. As previously indicated, in the post-Cold War era this phrase was largely side-tracked, which probably should not be surprising. While during the Cold War self-determination could be applied to self-determination of states – implying, for example, that Hungary should not be under Soviet control – a restricted application to states had become problematic by the time ethnic conflicts erupted. To recognise Yugoslavia's right to self-determination, then grant the same right to one of its republics is awkward, to say the least. Actually, that is precisely what happened. In the next chapter we shall focus on that specific case.

NOTES

1. Quoted in W. Ofuatey-Kodjoe, *The Principle of Self-Determination in International Law* (New York: Nellen Publishing Co, 1977) p. 98.
2. Memorandum to Myron C. Taylor, 1 September 1941. Papers of President Franklin D. Roosevelt, Secretary's File (Box 76), Hyde Park Library. Quoted in Ofuatey-Kodjoe, op. cit., p. 98.
3. Bennett Kovrig, 'Peacemaking after World War II: The End of the Myth of National Self-determination', in S. Borsody, ed., *The Hungarians: A Divided Nation* (New Haven: Yale Center for International and Area Studies, 1988) pp. 70–71.
4. Kovrig, ibid., pp. 75–76.
5. Ibid., p. 73.
6. The German-inhabited Sudeten region was also detached from Czechoslovakia in 1938 and reattached to Czechoslovakia – and its German inhabitants expelled – after the war.
7. The transfer was compulsory for a certain number of Hungarian collaborators with the Nazis.
8. Kalman Janics, 'The Hungarians in Slovakia', in Borsody, op. cit., p. 163.
9. Janics, ibid., p. 164.
10. The year 1968 was one of dramatic developments. The Slovak Dubcek became head of the Czechoslovak Communist Party and Czechoslovakia became a federation. However, Soviet troops entered Czechoslovakia and Dubcek was transferred to Moscow. Many of the reforms introduced by him were cancelled, but not the federal arrangement.
11. Ofuatey-Kodjoe, op. cit., p. 158.
12. E.H. Carr, *International Relations Between the Two World Wars, 1919–1939* (London: Macmillan, 1963) pp. 12–13.
13. Ofuatey-Kodjoe, op. cit., p. 85.
14. Ofuatey-Kodjoe, op. cit., p. 127.
15. Quoted in Ofuatey-Kodjoe, op. cit., p. 128.
16. Vol. 14 *I.L.M.* [International Legal Materials], [starting on page] 1292 (1975). The Conference opened in Helsinki, Finland, on 3 July 1973 and continued at Geneva, Switzerland, from 18 September 1973 to 21 July 1975. It was concluded in Helsinki on 1 August 1975. The Final Act was signed by representatives of 35 countries. Italics added to all quotations from the Final Act.
17. See for example, Allen Buchanan, 'Self-Determination and the Right to Secede', *Journal of International Affairs*, 45, 2 (Winter 1992) p. 349.
18. *I.L.M.* (1990). Signed in Paris on 21 November 1990, at the conclusion of a three-day summit meeting of the CSCE by heads of states of all European governments, except Albania, plus the United States and Canada.
19. *Conference on Yugoslavia Arbitration Commission: Opinions on Questions Arising from the Dissolution of Yugoslavia*, 31 *I.L.M.* 1488 (1992).

5   Yugoslavia: a case study

A keen observer of the situation in the former Yugoslavia has remarked:

> Before May 1991, Croats and Serbs lived together in relative content-
> ment throughout the regions which have now [in the summer of 1992]
> been so dreadfully ravaged. They were perfectly aware that the rotten
> ship of the Yugoslav state was entering troubled seas. Yet nobody in
> their wildest fantasy would have predicted that within a little more than
> twelve months, the peaceful town of Vukovar would be levelled to the
> ground in one of the most merciless bombardments of modern history.
> Nor would they have dreamed that Croat soldiers would massacre
> innocent Serbs, while Serb fighters would mutilate innocent Croats.[1]

This remark regarding relations between Croats and Serbs in
Croatia could also have been made about the Serb, Croat and Muslim
relations in Bosnia at least as late as December 1991, and possibly
even a month or two later. Bosnian Serbs, Bosnian Croats and
Bosnian Muslims also lived together in 'relative contentment
throughout the regions' that just a few months later were 'so dread-
fully ravaged'. The only part of Yugoslavia where violent ethnic
clashes occurred before 1991 was the southern Serbian province of
Kosovo, which will be discussed below.

SERBS AND CROATS

The evidence for 'deep antagonisms among the country's diverse
ethnic and religious groups'[2] long before the independence of the

later named Yugoslavia in 1918 is incontrovertible. Between the two world wars Yugoslavia was a centralised unitary state where the Orthodox Serbs dominated, and especially the Roman Catholic Croats felt 'deep antagonism' to what they perceived to be alien cultural domination.

This antagonism between Serbs and Croats erupted in particularly violent confrontations between them during World War II. Yugoslavia was occupied by Nazi German armies in April 1941 and partitioned. In Croatia a puppet government of the fascist Ustashi movement was set up, headed by Ante Pavelic. Subsequently, the Ustashi government declared the independence of Croatia, and its territory was unilaterally enlarged to include Bosnia and the territory and population which prior to independence in 1918 formed a part of Serbia. In sum, Nazi German troops occupied the territory of Yugoslavia and their fascist collaborators ruled in Croatia, now a separate state.

The resistance to Nazi occupation of Yugoslavia, including Croatia, was waged by the Partisans, or *Yugoslav* Partisans as they were then known, headed by Josip Broz Tito, a Croat and head of the Yugoslav Communist party. In their resistance the Partisans confronted the primarily Croat Ustashi – as well as the primarily Serb-nationalist, i.e., anti-communist, Chetniks. In these confrontations, the Ustashi massacred some 350,000 to 750,000 Serbs during the war, most of them civilians.[3] The Partisans also killed some 100,000, mostly uniformed fighters. The Serb-nationalist Chetniks in turn carried out the massacre of Croats and Bosnian Muslims, many of whom were also supporters of the Ustashi.

Croats and Serbs, including supporters of the Ustashi and supporters of the Partisans, also held opposite views as to the future structure of Yugoslavia. Probably all who were against the Nazis were committed to a unified Yugoslavia and were against 'balkanisation', while their opponents favoured an independent Croatia. At the end of the war the primarily Serb Partisans were the victors and the primarily Croat Ustashi the losers. In the years following the independence of the 'second' Yugoslavia in 1946 under Tito's leadership, many Croats continued to oppose what they perceived to be Serb political and cultural domination.

This opposition manifested itself in various ways but not in violent ethnic conflict. For example, a conference of Yugoslav intellectuals, writers, and artists – convened in 1954 with the intention of promoting cultural unity of Yugoslavia – was opposed by Croat participants. In 1967, 150 Croat intellectuals demanded that the Croat language and the Latin script of the Croats be accorded equal status with the Serb language and the Cyrillic script of the Serbs.[4] In the same period, Croat students demanded to be trained only in the Croat language while serving in the military after their studies, and to serve only in their own republic. By the late 1960s and the first years of the 1970s, Croat nationalists, unabashedly waving Ustashi symbols, demanded complete independence for Croatia. In 1972, Tito used the Yugoslav army to put down a 'counter-revolution' of the Croats;[5] the Croats perceived this as a Serb military action against them.

This brief account of Serb–Croat relations over the past several decades is intended to emphasise that the post-Cold War relations between Croats and Serbs was not merely between two religions and cultures but between two peoples bearing bitter memories.

BOSNIA

The ancestors of the inhabitants of today's Bosnia-Herzegovina were Serbs and Croats (thus Slavs), many of whom were converted to Islam by Muslim Ottoman (i.e. Turkish) conquerors during the first two centuries of Ottoman rule, which lasted from the fourteenth to the nineteenth centuries.

Conversion was more successful among Serb and Croat land-owners and local rulers who then became the rich middle and upper class city dwellers in Ottoman-ruled Bosnia-Herzegovina. The poor rural peasantry remained Orthodox Serb and Roman Catholic Croat. Thus emerged a religious as well as class distinction and antagonism among Southern Slavs inhabiting Bosnia-Herzegovina between Bosnian Orthodox-Serb and Bosnian Roman Catholic-Croat peasants on the one hand, and Bosnian-Muslims on the other hand. Furthermore, the Muslims of Bosnia-Herzegovina were seen by the rest of the population – and were officially considered to be – ethnically different Turks. The eventual result was the religious and ethnic mosaic that is now Bosnia-Herzegovina.

Bosnian Serb and Croat efforts to liberate Bosnia-Herzegovina
from Turkish rule also aimed at its liberation from Muslim rule. For
this purpose it was relatively easy for them to receive the support of
non-Bosnian Serbs (who remembered the Battle of Kosovo) and, to a
more limited degree, of non-Bosnian Croats. In fact, such a Serb
support of Bosnian-Serbs led, indirectly, to the independence of
Serbia. In support of Bosnian Serb and Bosnian Croat in the 1875–76
peasant uprisings against Ottoman rule, Serbia declared war on
Turkey in 1876. The badly beaten Serbs in the war that ensued were
saved by Austrian intervention on the Serbian side. When the
Russians declared war on Turkey in 1877, Serbians joined their anti-
Turk campaign which, for the Serbs, was in effect an anti-Bosnian-
Muslim campaign. After the conclusion of this war the Kingdom of
Serbia became independent in 1878. However, Bosnia-Herzegovina
was not included in the new Serbian state but was occupied by, and
in 1908 annexed to, Austria-Hungary. The annexation of Bosnia-
Herzegovina frustrated Serbian aspirations but satisfied non-Bosnian
Croatian aspirations, because Croatia, then part of Austria-Hungary,
also claimed Bosnia-Herzegovina.[6]

During World War I, the Serbian Karadjordevic dynasty and
other Serbian politicians continued to strive for the inclusion of
Bosnia-Herzegovina within the Serbian state. This did not happen.
Instead, there remained the dream of a Greater Serbia which, for
some, has lasted to this day; for other Serbs, was recently revived.
After the War, the Kingdom of Serbs, Croats and Slovenes was
created and existed as such until 1929, when it became Yugoslavia.

During World War II, Bosnia-Herzegovina was incorporated into
the independent state of Croatia by the fascist Croat regime and the
formerly Croat (converted) Muslims were declared to be 'Croats of
the Islamic faith'. Indeed, a majority of the Bosnian Muslims cooperated with the Croat fascist Ustashi, while Serbs in Bosnia tended
to support Tito's Partisans. As the war escalated, the Muslim
members of the Ustashi had carried out atrocities against the Serbs of
Bosnia that differed only in magnitude from Ustashi atrocities against
the non-Bosnian Serbs in Croatia.

In the 'second' Yugoslavia under Tito's rule (1946–91), '[T]he
largely Muslim communist ruling caste in Bosnia-Herzegovina ...
was noted for its particularly harsh, Stalinist pattern of internal rule,

despite the familiar trappings of "self-management socialism" which prevailed throughout Yugoslavia.'⁷ Nonetheless, bloody confrontations among antagonistic religious and ethnic groups – violent retribution – did not occur after the end of World War II on any significant scale and intensity either in Bosnia or elsewhere in Yugoslavia.

KOSOVO

The exception to the relatively peaceful relations among various groups in post-World War II Yugoslavia was the situation in Kosovo. Even there, major conflicts erupted only after Tito's death in 1980, when the overall situation worsened all over Yugoslavia. Ethnic Albanians particularly started to agitate against Serbs in Kosovo. In November 1987, David Binder of *The New York Times* reported 'hostilities ... [by] separatist-minded ethnic Albanians against the various Slavic populations of Yugoslavia ...'[8] He added that some ethnic Albanians saw as their goal to create an 'ethnic Albania that includes western Macedonia, southern Montenegro, part of southern Serbia, Kosovo, and Albania ...' while other ethnic Albanians 'admit a vision of a greater Albania governed from Pristina [Kosovo] ... rather than Tirana [Albania] ...'.

The same observer continued: 'In the last seven years 20,000 [Serbs and Montenegrans] have fled the [Kosovo] Province, often leaving behind farmsteads and houses, for safety in the Slavic north.' Kosovo was reported to have become an '"ethnically pure" Albanian region, a "Republic of Kosovo" in all but name.' The observer added: 'Last summer, the authorities in Kosovo said that they had documented 40 ethnic Albanian attacks on Slavs in two months.' *The New York Times* reported in the same 1987 article that 'in one incident, Fadil Hoxha, once the leading politician of ethnic Albanian origin in Yugoslavia, joked at an official dinner in Prizren last year that Serbian women should be used to satisfy potential ethnic Albanian rapists.' After this quip was reported, Serbian women in Kosovo protested and Mr Hoxha was dismissed from the Communist Party.

Another observer noted that '[U]ntil September [1987] the

majority of the Serbian Communist Party leadership [filled with younger political leaders], pursued a policy of seeking compromise with the Kosovo party hierarchy under its ethnic Albanian leader, Azem Vlasi.' But during a 30-hour session of the Serbian Central Committee in late September [1987] the Serbian Party Secretary, Slobodan Milosevic, deposed Dragisa Pavlovic as head of Belgrade's party organisation, accusing him of 'being an appeaser who was soft on Albanian radicals'. Milosevic called for 'the policy of the hard hand'. He said, 'We will go up against anti-Socialist forces, even if they call us Stalinists.'[9]

In sum, the ethnic and religious diversity of the peoples of Yugoslavia is well documented, as is the long history of confrontation between them. Croat dissatisfaction with the post-World War II federal arrangement of Yugoslavia was constant and especially vocal among expatriate Croats. Ustashi atrocities against the Serbs – and what the Croats perceived to be Serb atrocities against them – remained vivid memories. Nevertheless, although ethnic conflicts erupted in the Kosovo region almost immediately after Tito's death, there was no widespread, violent ethnic conflict elsewhere in Yugoslavia, even in the latter part of the 1980s. The question is, why? In other words: how was the minority problem handled in the former Yugoslavia under Tito?

'NATIONALITIES' IN TITO'S YUGOSLAVIA

It hardly needs to be restated that in post-World War II Yugoslavia – as in the Soviet Union then and earlier – authoritarian and repressive methods were used to control population and economy. It is a fact that in both countries political opposition and organisation were not tolerated and economic activities were centrally controlled. Populations in Yugoslavia – and the Soviet Union – had not enjoyed the political and economic freedoms their counterparts enjoyed in Western democracies.

It is also widely assumed that the relatively effective containment of ethnic conflicts and manifestations of extreme nationalism in communist-ruled Yugoslavia – and in the Soviet Union – are also due to the above-listed facts. In other words, it is assumed that the repressive, centralised methods of rule used by *communist regimes* in political, economic, social, and cultural spheres were responsible for the decades-long virtual absence of large-scale ethnic conflicts within Yugoslavia – and the Soviet Union. To put it in still another way, it is widely believed that *communist regimes* were capable of preventing ethnic conflicts.

This widely held assumption, which has had great influence on assessments of the origins of ethnic conflict and ways of its prevention and reduction, requires closer scrutiny.

Authoritarian and repressive methods of governments, and centralised control of the economy are *regime attributes*; they characterise the way of doing things, the methods and style of a governmental and administrative machinery. Democratic methods, allowing freedoms in the various spheres of life, are also regime attributes, albeit basically the opposite ones. It is proposed that a state, any state, also has a *structural*, or organisational set-up, or attribute. This was true of Yugoslavia and the Soviet Union, as well as the United States, Nigeria and elsewhere. Structural attributes of any state must also be examined.

To illustrate the distinction between regime and structural attributes let us take Germany as an example. The *regime* in today's Germany is democratic, that is, there is freedom to organise, to participate in elections, engage in economic activities, and so on. But any assessment of political and economic conditions in Germany should also take into account the fact that, *structurally*, it is a federal system and, in addition, also a member of the European Union.

The proposition is that the structural attributes of Germany – its internal organisation and its membership in a wider framework – may be as responsible for the political and economic conditions in Germany today as the fact that elections are held, that freedom of the press prevails. Thus, the structural attributes of Yugoslavia – and the Soviet Union which we shall not focus on – may also be as responsible for the containment of extreme nationalism during the rule of Tito as its regime attributes. To what degree is an open question.

First among the structures in Yugoslavia was the single party. Please note, the emphasis here is on the *number*, not on the ideological or other programmatic content. The emphasis is on the fact that no political organisations rivalling that single party were allowed to function in Yugoslavia – nor in the Soviet Union. Thus absent was the most commonly used instrument for the attainment of political power through ethnic mobilisation. Prospective political entrepreneurs either had to pursue a political career in the single party, leave the country (as, for example, many Croats did), or submit to arrests and jailing.

Second among the structures was the federal system. In Yugoslavia – and to a degree in the Soviet Union – the federal system was built around specific nationalities. Each structural component, each republic of the federation, was given a considerable degree of autonomy. However, political power in each autonomous entity was in the hands of the dominant nationality in principle and, when possible, in practice. Such an autonomy arrangement left other nationalities, or ethnic groups, in these political units at the mercy of the dominant group and could have prompted or promoted conflict. But, in Yugoslavia – and in the Soviet Union – the exercise of authority and power in the hands of dominant groups in the respective autonomous republics was overseen and curtailed by the political party and federal institutions in Belgrade – and Moscow. Thus, Serbs in Croat dominated Croatia, for example, could count on the party and the central government in Belgrade to control and curtail government excesses toward them in Croatia.

The third among the structures was the economic system. From the regime perspective, the economy was centrally controlled and largely owned, and no economic activity could be undertaken, in principle, without permission from the centre. From the structural perspective, the economies of the autonomous republics of Yugoslavia were interdependent components of the wide economic framework of Yugoslavia.[10] By a 'wide economic framework' is meant, primarily, a wide human and material resource pool, an interlocking network of production, an absence of customs and tariffs, and secured markets. Thus, favourable economic conditions – such as full employment – are not attributable to the (communist) *regime* – at least not to it alone – but (also) to the existence of the wide economic framework, that is, the *structure*. The inverse is also true.

In sum, the three structural attributes that must be taken into consideration in assessing the relatively successful long-term containment of ethnic conflicts and extreme nationalism in Yugoslavia and in the Soviet Union are these: (1) the single-party structure which bars opportunities for rival political mobilisation, including ethno-political mobilisation; (2) a federal structure built around dominant ethnic groups/nationalities, providing centralised control of the power of dominant groups over minorities; and (3) a wide economic framework that encloses ample resources and secure markets.

Again, the apparent positive structural aspects of countries do not substitute for the evidently negative aspects of their regimes. In the Yugoslav – and the Soviet – federal arrangements personal freedoms were curtailed; individuals who deviated from the dominant and dominating political ideology were restrained and repressed; private entrepreneurship was curtailed. These and other measures were attributes of their regimes. But it is due to structural attributes that prospective political entrepreneurs had no venues for the mobilisation of citizens on the basis of their ethnic identity.

THE EFFECT OF DEMOCRATISATION IN THE YUGOSLAV FEDERATION

The introduction of *glasnost* and *perestroika* in the Soviet Union in 1987 prompted an overall process of liberalisation in the eastern European Soviet orbit and in Yugoslavia, while the 'democratic earthquake that rocked eastern Europe in the fall of 1989',[11] launched 'democratisation'. The process of democratisation in Yugoslavia affected the three structural attributes in three distinct, though at times overlapping, phases, which we shall now list and elaborate on.

The first phase affected the single-party structure. In this first phase, political parties started to get organised and preparations were made for participation in hastily arranged elections. Scores of political entrepreneurs set out to mobilise followers and voters around a variety of party platforms and political slogans. Many among these aspiring political leaders set out to mobilise followers around ethnic or, as it was commonly referred to, national identity. Also, at this initial phase of heated competition among themselves, political entrepreneurs did make declarations about 'independence' and 'disassociation' from Yugoslavia. But there were no calls as yet for secession. Religious differences, cultural cleavages and historical memories did play important roles in this phase of democratic competition for power, but the budding 'ethnic nationalism' did not yet aim at sovereign statehood.[12] From the collapse of the Berlin Wall in November 1989, which symbolised the 'democratic earthquake', to December 1991, negotiations in the former Yugoslavia strove toward a reform of the federation, that is to say, revising the relationship between autonomous more-or-less national entities and the political centre in Belgrade. In this first phase, ethnic nationalism – national sentiments of 'minorities' in the various republics of the federation – did not produce the kind of violent acts later referred to as 'ethnic cleansing'.

The second phase affected the federal structure, and emerged as the rhetorical slogans of independence gradually undermined attempts at reforming the federation and as the independence of the member republics became a political goal. In other words, if those who favoured an internal restructuring of the Yugoslav federation had been successful – and with appropriate external support of that cause they probably could have been – widespread ethnic conflict might have been prevented despite the overall ethnic diversity and traditional hostilities. Ethnic tensions worsened and violent ethnic conflict erupted when the break-up of the federation became a virtual certainty; in Croatia, when independence was clearly looming on the horizon, and in Bosnia-Herzegovina when recognition of the breakaway state as an independent entity actually occurred.

In this second phase, political authority (the right to rule) and political power (the capacity to rule) were about to be transferred, or were actually transferred, from the distant federal capital, Belgrade, to the capitals of new *unitary and centralised* states. From the perspective of 'minorities' in the former republics of the federation, this meant the disappearance of the long-distance party and government control from the federal centre; it meant the end of the previously existing possibility of curtailing the powers of dominant groups within autonomous entities of the federal arrangement. 'Minorities' were left with internal and international assurances that human rights would be respected, including the ones we referred to in the previous chapter.

Such assurances could hardly neutralise the perceived threat that the prospective direct control by the governments of the future independent, centralised, unitary states posed to the 'minority' ethnic groups within them. To put it differently, international assurances of democracy and protection of human rights in the future probably could not erase the memories of pre-World War II undemocratic behaviour, belligerence, and disrespect for human rights on the part of dominant groups. Thus, Serbs in Croatia, for example, feared that the sovereign independence of Croatia would 'leave them at the political mercy of a Croatian majority and a [Croatian] nationalist government'.[13] That nationalist government was seen by them as a revived Ustashi government.

The third phase affects the wide economic framework that in Yugoslavia enclosed ample resources and secure markets. This phase is only relevant to Slovenia, whose population experienced only a very brief war.[14] In the other new states emerging from Yugoslavia, economic decline and deprivation can still be attributed to the conflict and also to economic sanctions. After the conflict, governments of the new states will be able rightly to blame the conflict for economic dislocations. However, the fact is, that instead of being members in a wide economic framework, there emerged five or six states, each with far fewer resources and more limited internal markets than the ones they had as members of the Yugoslav federation. Of course, all of them will be hoping for membership in the European Union, the same as other Central European states do, and for the same purpose of being again a member in a wide economic framework. Let us turn now to the dynamics of change.

FROM A BUDDING 'CIVIL SOCIETY' TO ETHNIC CONFLICT

During the 1980s, after the death of Tito in 1980, a relative ethnic peace prevailed in Yugoslavia, except in Kosovo. Even in the late 1980s the population was primarily concerned with the Yugoslav economy and the political elite, with its planned centralisation as a way of revitalising it. In a book published in 1992, and researched and written a year or two earlier, Robert F. Miller, a seasoned

observer of Yugoslavia, foresaw in the changing Yugoslavia of the
late 1980s the emergence of a civil society. He saw nationalism and
ethnic awakening not as threats but as possible factors in the formation
of such a society:

> Developments in Yugoslavia in the past two years offer many useful
> insights into the structure and behaviour of civil societies emerging
> throughout the former socialist world. In particular, they illustrate
> the powerful impact of nationalism on the kinds of civil societies that
> emerge. Where nationalism is especially strong, the conduct of newly
> formed popular movements may take on an unattractively self-
> indulgent colouration, directed against the rights and personal
> security of alien ethnic and social groups. This may well turn out to be
> only a stage in the evolution of a socially functional civil society.[15]

The political climate had started to change, and the Yugoslav
society began to stray off the road leading toward a 'civil society' in
1990 which, one must note, was after the crumbling of the Berlin
Wall in November 1989. The first stage consisted of preparations for
the multi-party elections which were held in all republics of Yugoslavia from April to December 1990. Some 200 political parties were
formed. The agendas of some of these parties no longer included only
demands for democratisation of the political system and economic
reforms to revitalise the economic system. The implementation of
these reforms was taken for granted. The agendas also included
demands for reforming the federal system.

This reasonable demand was, nevertheless, risky. A failure of
reaching a consensus on reforming the federation – which meant, at a
minimum, the rearrangement of relations among the republics and
the federal government and, at maximum, converting the federation
into a confederation – could automatically have meant seceding from
it: that, however, with a caveat. From the time of elections in 1990 to
the end of 1991 secession was an option in only two republics of
Yugoslavia: Slovenia and Croatia. Bosnia and Macedonia were not
yet on the agenda, at least not as obviously, and the sixth republic,
Montenegro, was not even slated to be.

The 1990 elections in Slovenia produced a non-communist government, and its parliament declared Slovenia's sovereignty – but not its

secession from Yugoslavia. 'The goal is not to break Yugoslavia apart but for Slovenia to link itself with the new order in Europe', said Iztok Simoniti, a spokesman for the republic's Secretariat of Foreign Affairs. Nevertheless, '[I]f we aren't able to find a common language in Yugoslavia, secession is not out of the question.'[16] In the summer of 1990, a noted scholar remarked:

'few in Slovenia ... expected or really desired a total rupture with the rest of Yugoslavia. There was a general recognition that the Slovenian economy was almost inextricably tied to the Yugoslav economy and had a ready and profitable market for its goods there that would be difficult to replace elsewhere in the world, given the cost and quality characteristics of Slovenian products and the relatively low prices of domestic fuels and raw materials.'[17]

Indeed, in 1990, the new government of Slovenia – and of Croatia – proposed the transformation of the Yugoslav federation of six republics into a confederation of sovereign states and threatened to 'dissociate' from the federation only if the planned negotiations did not result in a confederal arrangement. The Yugoslav government in Belgrade, in turn, drafted proposals for changes in the federal Constitution that were intended to convert Yugoslavia into a 'modern and efficient state of laws'. 'The proposal ... calls for political pluralism, the codification of guarantees of civil and individual freedoms and curtailment of the dominant position of the Communist party, which is named the League of Communists.'[18] In September of 1990, a new Constitution was adopted in **Serbia**, which was to guarantee human rights and a multi-party system.[19]

In **Croatia**, multi-party elections of 1990 brought Franjo Tudjman, a former general in Tito's army, to the presidency of the Yugoslav Republic of Croatia. For Tudjman, Croatia, attaining independence was only a matter of time; negotiations about federal reforms merely tactics. Tudjman stated as early as 4 April 1990: 'We have played democracy for long enough and it is high time to say that Croatia is a republic and that it has the right to establish order.'[20] A few weeks later, in May, he openly threatened the secession of Croatia from Yugoslavia.

The eventual independence of Croatia was to be far more problematic than the eventual independence of Slovenia. Slovenia was ethnically homogeneous. Croatia was not; it had a sizable Serb population, constituting about 12 per cent of Croatia's population. The Serbs clearly demonstrated by their feet that they were not willing to remain a minority in an independent Croatia. In the summer of 1990, Serbs in the largely Serbian region of Krajina, south of Zagreb, began an insurgency. In September 1990, there was again a weekend of unrest during which Croatian police began confiscating weapons from Yugoslav police-stations and Yugoslav militia-units (manned primarily by Serbs) in Serb-dominated areas of Croatia. Feeling threatened, Serbs in Croatia held a referendum on Serbian autonomy, where any Serb born or living in Croatia was allowed to vote. Subsequently, Serbs declared themselves 'autonomous' in the predominantly Serbian counties of Croatia.

President Tudjman opposed the Serbian claim to autonomy. In his eyes, Serbs in Croatia had no right to it. In his view, Croatian Serbs, especially in the Krajina region, should accept Croatia's independence and constitution, that is, a unitary state. Why was Tudjman so adamant about Croatia's independence, how *could* he be so adamant about it?[21]

For one, the Croatian Democratic Community (HDZ), Tudjman's party, received considerable financial support from Croatian emigrants around the world – especially the United States, Australia and Canada. Many among these Croat expatriates were themselves, or were the descendants of those members of the Ustashi who left with the defeated Nazi German forces at the end of World War II. These expatriate Croats insisted on Croatia's secession from Yugoslavia, that is, freeing Croats from domination by Serbs, whom they fought, and massacred many, during World War II. On 10 May 1991 a paid advertisement appeared in *The New York Times* with the title 'Croatian democracy must prevail'. The advertisement was in the form of an open letter from the 'Croatian Democratic Union of America' and 'United Croatian Youth of America' and addressed to the President, Congress, and 'our fellow Americans . . .:

> We, Croatian-Americans, appeal to you to support the democratically elected government of the [independent] Republic of Croatia and its [future] President Franjo Tudman [*sic*] in this time of crisis . . .

The United States should support the territorial integrity of the [independent] Republic of Croatia and the rights of Croatian people to decide their own future, including their right to self-determination.

This expatriate insistence on Croatia's independence also sustained the expectation of Tudjman and his followers that the Croat expatriates could provide, would provide, or otherwise have access to funds for economic development in independent Croatia.

What was the policy of Belgrade toward secession? Cohen wrote:

> Milosevic's position on the future of the Serbs in Croatia and elsewhere was clear: . . . he did not oppose the self-determination of Yugoslavia's nations, or even legal secession by the republics, as long as those rights did not infringe on the equal rights of Serbs in a particular republic to exercise self-determination. Accordingly, Milosevic maintained, if a majority of citizens in Croatia or Bosnia, for example, desired their independence from the Yugoslav state, the borders of those republics must be changed in order to protect the interest of local Serb inhabitants.[22]

This was the stated position of Milosevic. Whether he meant it or not, whether he would have abided by it or not, are unanswerable questions. It seems to be, however, a fact that foreign governments, which could have held Milosevic faithful to his words, have not done so.

Demands for reforming the federation and the alternative secession posed a serious challenge to foreign policies of Western powers. All of them supported democratisation and economic reform. On these two issues policies were clear-cut. On the other hand, foreign policies regarding changes in the federal system were not so clear-cut. There was a principled overall commitment to the territorial integrity of Yugoslavia. President Bush of the United States and the President of the European Community, Jacques Delors, asserted in 1990, and for almost the next two years, that they would not support the break-up of Yugoslavia. In July of 1990, *The New York Times* reported: 'The United States supports Yugoslavia's unity and territorial integrity and maintains that is up to the Yugoslavs to work out their relationships.' But, 'to work out their relationships' was too ambiguous a phrase to extend to it unreserved commitment which thus weakened their commitment to the territorial integrity of Yugoslavia and enhanced the disintegrative forces in it.

Intensive negotiations were taking place among the leaders of various republics between January and June of 1991 on a possible confederal arrangement in Yugoslavia. As late as 21 June 1991, the United States Secretary of State, James Baker, on an official visit in Belgrade, again expressed the United States government's opposition to secession. In the same month, Franjo Tudjman, still President of the Yugoslav Republic of Croatia, declared Croatia's independence. Serbs working in the Croat government were dismissed, and before the end of the month, the Slovenian government declared independence.

The Yugoslav army attempted to prevent the separation of Slovenia from the Yugoslav federation in a six-day-long, and unsuccessful, military campaign. The Yugoslav army – including Serbian militia and irregulars – withdrew from Slovenia, then seized control of a third of the separatist Republic of Croatia, the area where mostly Serbs lived. Six months of violent conflicts ensued between Croatian forces and Serbs in Croatia supported by the Yugoslav army. Attempts at ending the fighting failed. Stephen Engelberg reported in *The New York Times* in December, 1991:

> Even if Mr. Milosevic [the President of Serbia] eventually agrees to a peace treaty, it is not clear that the Serbs in Krajina region and elsewhere [in Croatia] will follow. Two Serbian regions in Croatia have already declared themselves independent republics.[23]

By the end of 1991, Western powers were about to change policies. The German government took the lead in insisting on recognising Croatia, a traditional German ally. It is not clear whether German sympathisers of fascist Croatia or German weapons exporters had greater influence. It is quite clear, however, that rhetorical references to moral principles were no more than a smoke screen and that the German government was interested specifically in the independence of Croatia. Engelberg's report continued:

> Bonn prodded its more reluctant allies in the 12 nation European

Community to agree to recognise by January 15, 1992 any inde-
pendence-minded Yugoslav republic that respects human rights,
established borders and the peaceful arbitration of differences. ...
The German foreign Minister Hans-Dietrich Genscher has argued
that sanctions against Serbia, coupled with diplomatic recognition of
Croatia, and the political support it implies, will slow or stop the
violence.

In other Western capitals there still prevailed the view in December
1991 that '... the war could worsen as a result of Germany's
successful campaign to extend diplomatic recognition to Croatia and
Slovenia ...' There was still a concern that recognition 'could prompt
the Yugoslav Army to begin a fresh offensive before Croatia imports
new weapons, or could lead to new clashes in Bosnia and Herzegovina,
the republic that shares borders with Croatia and Serbia'.

Then, the Bosnian government announced on 20 December 1991,
that it would also seek independence, which the already armed
elements of the Serb minority in the Bosnia-Herzegovina declared
they would not accept. However, by January of 1992 the Rubicon
was crossed, and the die was cast. The European Community
recognised the independence of Slovenia and Croatia.

The same month, January 1992, Bosnia-Herzegovina was still not
recognised by Western powers as an independent state. In a Lisbon
meeting at the end of February 1992, three Bosnian leaders representing their respective groups – Bosnian-Muslims, Bosnian-Serbs
and Bosnian-Croats – endorsed a proposal that Bosnia-Herzegovina
be a confederation of three ethnic regions. Mr Izetbegovic's acceptance of the proposal, which would have denied him and his Muslim
party whom he represented a dominant role in the Bosnian republic,
surprised not only his supporters at home, but also United States
policy makers. David Binder wrote in *The New York Times*:

Immediately after Mr. Izetbegovic returned from Lisbon, Mr.
Zimmerman [the US Ambassador to Yugoslavia] called on him in
Sarajevo. The Bosnian leader complained bitterly that the European
Community and Bosnian Serbs and Croats had pressured him to
accept partition. 'He said he didn't like it,' Mr Zimmerman recalled.
'I told him, if he didn't like it, why sign it?' In retrospect, Mr.

Zimmerman said in a recent interview, 'the Lisbon agreement wasn't bad at all.' But, after talking to the Ambassador, Mr. Izetbegovic publicly renounced the Lisbon agreement.[24]

The developments that followed this meeting between Mr Izetbegovic and Mr Zimmerman, the Ambassador of the United States, are crucial for an understanding of the circumstances that led to the eruption of the bloody conflict in Bosnia-Herzegovina.

There were clear indications of Bosnian Serb opposition to the independence of Bosnia-Herzegovina and repeated warnings of its consequences. In a referendum in Bosnia-Herzegovina, concluded on 1 March 1992, Muslims and Croats chose the independence option, while the 1.2 million Serbs of Bosnia boycotted the referendum. To underline this opposition, Serbian 'irregulars, backed by Yugoslav Army contingents, clashed with Muslim and Croatian forces in Bosnia and Herzegovina in what diplomats called a clear attempt to block European Community recognition of the republic's independence.'[25]

In early March 1992, talks about the possible partitioning of Bosnia reconvened in Brussels. Would Serb militants have accepted the partitioning of Bosnia in March 1992? Could large-scale violence have been prevented? We shall never know. On 8 or 9 March, United States Secretary of State James Baker urged in a meeting with European Foreign Ministers to recognise Mr Izetbegovic's government of Bosnia-Herzegovina immediately. A week later, Dr Karadzic, representing the Bosnian Serbs at another meeting of the three Bosnian leaders in Sarajevo, warned of 'a civil war between ethnic groups and religions with hundreds of thousands of deaths and hundreds of towns destroyed' if the independence of Bosnia-Herzegovian were recognised. The next day the three leaders did sign a new agreement to divide Bosnia into 'three constituent units' based on ethnic criteria. In other words, according to that agreement, if Bosnia-Herzegovina were to become independent it would not be a unitary state. Two days later, on 8 March it was Mr Izetbegovic who voiced strong reservations about the agreement. Nonetheless, by the end of the month diplomatic negotiations did take place in Brussels to draw the map of partition.

As late as 3 April 1992, the Yugoslav presidency warned the

European Community not to recognise the Bosnian republic's independence. 'The government will inform the European Community and other international factors about the serious consequences that could result if the European Community recognises Bosnia and Herzegovina's independence', the statement said.

To no avail. Two days later, on 5 April 1992, 12 European Community Foreign Ministers announced the recognition by their countries of the independence of Bosnia and Herzegovina. At once, President Bush also recognised, not a partitioned Bosnia but 'the sovereignty of the Sarajevo government [in Bosnia] as well as the independence of Croatia and Slovenia'. According to the President, this recognition was extended in an attempt to head-off the partitioning of the republic, which, in the United States' government's view, would almost certainly result in a bloodbath because the ethnic groups were so intermeshed.

A peaceful resolution of inter-ethnic tensions may have been possible if Western foreign policies had continued to endorse, and insist upon, reforming the federation. Such an insistence was weak or altogether absent. Ultimately, the shift in foreign policies away from commitment to the territorial integrity of Yugoslavia towards recognition of breakaway states exacerbated the conflict rather than prevented it. The bloodbath that President Bush mentioned was not prevented by recognition; it followed it.

ETHNIC CONFLICT AND 'ETHNIC CLEANSING' IN
BOSNIA-HERZEGOVINA

Violent clashes erupted immediately after the international recognition of Bosnia-Herzegovina as an independent state. *The New York Times* reported on 10 April 1992:

> Well over 100 people have been killed in Bosnia and Herzegovina since its slide into civil war began last week just as the republic was gaining recognition from the European Community and the United States.[26]

Serbia (including Vojvodina and Kosovo) and Montenegro – whose populations voted to remain part of Yugoslavia – proclaimed themselves on 26 April 1992 to be the new Yugoslav state. The Yugoslav government, that is, Milosevic, also declared that 'the new Yugoslavia has "no territorial claims" on its neighbouring republics ...'[27]

This declaration fell on deaf ears. Western policies were already set. Slovenia, Croatia and Bosnia-Herzegovina were recognised as independent unitary states, and those who aimed at disrupting the territorial integrity of these independent states, Serbs, did have 'terrritorial claims' in the eyes of Western governments. In Bosnia-Herzegovina one of the most violent confrontations in the post-Cold War era had already erupted. The only question remaining was how to call this conflict: ethnic conflict? civil war? Both terms were set aside and superseded by a new term. The phrase 'ethnic cleansing' emerged as the one that could, and did, not only become a focus for policy formulation but also could, and did, ally world public opinion in support of foreign policies.

The phrase 'ethnic cleansing' is not in the Oxford Dictionary of the English language. As far as could be ascertained through systematic computer search, the phrase 'ethnic cleansing' was not used in English prior to 1991, either in news materials or in published scholarly writings. There was one exception.

The one exception was noted by the American columnist William Safire, whose articles appear regularly in *The New York Times*. He devoted his column in *The New York Times Magazine* of 14 March 1993 to 'Ethnic Cleansing' and in that column he wrote that '[i]n 1988, well before the Soviet Union came apart, clashes broke out between Armenians and Azerbidjanis in the autonomous enclave of Azerbidjan known as Nagorno-Karabakh.' Safire then remarked that 'according to Sol Steinmetz, executive editor of Random House dictionaries, who cites Serbo-Croatian sources, the attempt by one group to drive out the other was called by Soviet officials *etnicheskoye chishcheniye*, "ethnic cleansing".'

Significantly, the phrase was not repeated in public at the time; there was no mention of it in either journalistic or scholarly writings in connection with the Armenian-Azerbidjani conflict, or in any other connection. Safire did mention in his article that a Serbian building supervisor named Zarko Cubrilo told Tim Judah, a *Times* of London reporter on 9 July 1991: 'Many of us have been sacked because they [the Croats] want an *ethnically clean* Croatia.' Safire also mentioned John F. Burns of *The New York Times*, who on 26 July 1992 described the movement for a 'Greater Serbia' and that 'the precondition for its creation lies in the purging – "ethnic cleansing" in the perpetrators' lexicon – of wide areas of Bosnia of all but like-minded Serbs.' Safire asserted in his column that '[t]hat is the first take at a big phrase . . .'

Not quite. The first documented use of the phrase 'ethnic cleansing' was in a report by Donald Forbes of Reuters News Agency on 13 July 1991. Mr Forbes quoted in his report a spokesman of the Croat Supreme Council:

> The aim of this expulsion [of Croats by Serbs in Croatia] is obviously the ethnic cleansing of the critical areas . . . to be annexed to Serbia.

True, the phrase was not repeated in print for the rest of 1991. Newspapers did not pick it up. But some five months later, on 2 January 1992, the *USA Today* reported that one Major Cheko, a Serbian 'warlord' operating from Pejlevja, Montenegro, led 'ethnic cleansing attacks' on Muslims in eastern Bosnia.[28]

Three weeks later, on 25 January 1992, the BBC reported that Mate Granic, spokesman for the Croatian government, demanded the disbandment of the Yugoslav army. He was reported as saying:

> Recently in the Knin, Crnis and Vukovar areas and in Baranja we have had processes of ethnic 'cleansing', that is, the aggressor is applying terror in an attempt to expel all the Croats from these areas.[29]

The next mention of the phrase was made some three months later, on 13 May 1992. Chuck Sudetic reported for *The New York Times* from Sarajevo that 'residents talk fearfully of a final attack and of campaigns of "ethnic cleansing" efforts by which extremist Serbs wish to intimidate and expel all but their ethnic kin from mixed neighborhoods . . .' Until 13 May 1992 the phrase was printed in the media four times during a period of ten months, between 13 July 1991 and 13 May 1992.

The phrase finally entered the vocabulary on 14 May 1992 when the United States Department of State spokesperson, Ms Margaret Tutwiler, used it. After Ms Tutwiler had mentioned it, the phrase appeared hundreds of times in the pages of printed media in the United States and elsewhere. The uttering of the phrase 'ethnic cleansing' by the official spokesperson of the State Department was enough to legitimise it.

Here then is the step-by-step description of the birth of the phrase on a single occasion, when Margaret Tutwiler mentioned the phrase, in a very circumscribed way one might add, in a long (4185 word) briefing to reporters:

Margaret Tutwiler: We are concerned about reports that Serb forces
  there [in Bosnia] have begun to remove non-Serbs in an ethnic,
  quote, 'cleansing', unquote, operation.
One of the reporters then posed a question: Margaret, what did you
  mean, an 'ethnic cleansing operation'? Do you have any more
  details on that?
Ms. Tutwiler: Well, I'd ask the people who are putting out that.
  That's their phrase.
Question: Whose quotes?
Ms. Tutwiler: That's why I used quotes.
Question: So, it's their quotes?
Ms. Tutwiler: Correct.
Question: You have no other details on what's going on in that regard?
Ms. Tutwiler: No, I don't have any details of it. It is obviously a –
  well, I won't put an adjective on it. You do that.[30]

Margaret Tutwiler did not say 'ethnic cleansing'. She was careful in saying 'ethnic, quote, "cleansing", unquote, operation.' When she was asked to clarify what she meant by 'ethnic cleansing operation' she, again, did not elaborate but referred the questioner to 'the people who are putting out that. That's their phrase.' Nonetheless, the phrase uttered by the spokesperson of the State Department was enough to propel it into common usage.

The next day, 15 May 1992, the British *The Daily Telegraph* in a leading article wrote:

So far, 650,000 Muslims have been driven from their ancestral homes,
victims of a campaign openly described by Serb authorities as *ciscenje*
– ethnic cleansing. In its latest report, the UN describes it as 'a

concerted effort by the Serbs of Bosnia, with the acquiescence of, and at least some support from, the Yugoslav National Army to create "pure" regions.'

Five days after the press conference of Ms Tutwiler, on 19 May 1992, Haris Silajdzic, the Foreign Minister of Bosnia-Herzegovina, spoke at the National Press Club, Washington, DC. In his talk he said that 'international observers must be deployed to occupied towns in an effort to stop ethnic cleansing through forced expulsion, and a lasting ceasefire must be implemented . . .'

Question: We've heard – you used the term ethnic cleansing. We've heard that numerous times.
Minister Silajdzic: Yes.
Question: Could you explain exactly what that means?
Minister Siladjzic: Ethnic cleansing means that the aggressive forces are driving out the populations of Bosnia-Herzegovina, non-Serbian population out of their homes, villages, towns.[31]

The meaning of the phrase evolved gradually. When the phrase was used in the United States in early 1992, 'ethnic cleansing' referred to a policy of creating ethnically homogeneous regions. The implementation of the policy of 'ethnic cleansing' was seen to involve transfer of populations and the use of force to carry out the transfer. It clearly had negative connotations; but, the evidence seems to show that the phrase did not initially refer to loss of human life. It was first objected to as a morally condemnable policy, plan, or intent. Only somewhat later did the phrase connote rape and murder. Or, to put it differently and probably more accurately, rape and murder were later covered by the phrase 'ethnic cleansing' alongside the policy of creating ethnically homogeneous regions through expulsion and population transfer. In addition, 'ethnic cleansing' had come not only to clarify the nature of that conflict as objectionable, it also pointed to a new post-Cold War enemy, the Serbs, as its virtually exclusive perpetrators.

The usage of the phrase 'ethnic cleansing' declined from the latter part of 1993 on, but its frequent use during the first stages of the conflict in Bosnia-Herzegovina was helpful for foreign policy makers.

True, the mere recognition of Bosnia-Herzegovina as an independent state may have been a sufficient excuse to regard the conflict as an internal affair of a sovereign state and to support its territorial integrity. However, the sudden shift from supporting the territorial integrity of Yugoslavia to foreign governments supporting, in fact, secession, could have been contested. Foreign policy makers did not have a clear-cut and fully defendable case. Then, first, the atrocious crimes committed in the process of 'ethnic cleansing' drew attention away from the policy to the act itself. Second, the dominant opinion that these acts were committed by Serbs in the service of the Serb aspiration for a Greater Serbia, also cast the recognition of Bosnia-Herzegovina as a legitimate policy move to prevent its absorption by the Serbs.

RECAPITULATION

It was not the purpose of this chapter to provide a detailed account of the break-up of Yugoslavia. We focused on Yugoslavia because of the saliency of events there, because the conflict that followed its break-up was deemed useful in understanding the challenge that 'an ethnic mosaic' poses in Central Europe and elsewhere, and because it appeared as a fitting case from which to extrapolate hypotheses on the origins of ethnic conflict. We shall elaborate on a hypothesis in Part II. It seems appropriate to hint at it already here.

The eruption of bloody conflict in the former Yugoslavia has been widely attributed by policy makers, journalists and scholars alike to ethnic antagonism, ethnic grievances, and to the fact that 'deep-seated ethnic resentments persisted, simmering beneath the facade of stability and cohesion'.[32] Indeed, memories of atrocities committed before and during World War II were probably not forgotten by survivors and their descendants. But, since there were no large-scale violent eruptions of ethnic conflicts for over 40 years, it seems inappropriate to establish a cause-and-effect relationship between 'deep-seated ethnic resentments' and ethnic conflict. Consequently, one may legitimately pose a series of pertinent questions: Why did violent ethnic conflict not erupt in Croatia until the autumn of 1991 and in Bosnia-Herzegovina not until the spring of 1992? Since hostile attitudes were not new, why had violent ethnic conflicts not erupted – with the possible exception of events in Kosovo which may fall into such a category – since 1946?

One of the often cited responses to these questions is that Tito's authoritarian communist rule repressed all potential nationalist and ethnic manifestations. According to this view, ethnic hatred was simply unleashed at the end of Tito's regime.

The difficulty with such a view is that Tito died in 1980 and violent ethnic conflicts erupted not soon after his death but, except in Kosovo, over a decade after his death. In addition, although Tito's rule may have actually been authoritarian and repressive – and to a considerable degree it was – the absence of violent ethnic conflicts in Yugoslavia is attributed to his communist style centralisation of power in hindsight. When Tito was alive, his deeds were appreciated rather than criticised in the West. His policies toward 'nationalities' in Yugoslavia were either acceptable to the Western world, including the United States, or were disregarded by it. A former Eastern Europe and Moscow Bureau chief of the *Washington Post* noted:

> For most Americans, [Yugoslavia] was a place of quarrelling and obscure ethnic groups who were welded together by the great communist heretic Marshal Josip Broz Tito. Americans admired the Tito image: a courageous rebel who defied the Goliath Stalin and abandoned suffocating Soviet-style policies in favor of a kinder, gentler communism. The United States ... poured billions of dollars into Tito's treasury.[33]

It is true that ethnic conflict has erupted after the introduction of competitive elections – which are seen as the antithesis to repressive communist rule. But competitive elections were introduced a decade after Tito's death, in 1990. To argue that the Communist Party continued to be the single party during these ten years and that in itself, not Tito's rule *per se*, was responsible for repressive rule, is little more than an attempt to ignore the fact that not merely repression ended in 1990 but freedom was then extended to organise political parties which, in turn, provided the licence for ethnic mobilisation.

As to ethnic antagonism as a cause of conflict, there is no evidence that conflicts in Croatia and Bosnia-Herzegovina erupted *because* of it. All one can say with a considerable degree of certainty is that the brutality that followed the eruption of conflict was due to already existing antagonism, to the intensity of memories of past atrocities.

Lastly, there is the argument that Serbs have long been dreaming about a Greater Serbia, and the Yugoslav army was sent into Slovenia, Croatia and Bosnia-Herzegovina in order to create that Greater Serbia. It is indisputable that the Yugoslav army waged a five- to ten-day war in Slovenia, fought in Croatia, and participated and logistically supported the Bosnian Serbs. However, the following facts should also be taken into consideration: (1) Human rights of Serbs in Croatia were curtailed by the government of the still not independent Croatia, at least since 1990. One may find at least *some* legitimacy in the Yugoslav army's intervention on behalf of Serb citizens in the still federated Yugoslavia; (2) Serbs in Bosnia-Herzegovina boycotted the referendum on the independence of Bosnia-Herzegovina which they clearly did not desire and were willing to resist – especially with help from the Yugoslav army.

These facts do not imply that the dream of Greater Serbia did not exist; they might merely imply that Yugoslav army interventions in the republics were not primarily aimed at realising that dream.

If neither the end of repression caused the eruption of ethnic conflict, nor antagonism, nor memory of past atrocities; if not the Yugoslav army instigated conflict but only assisted one side in the conflict, then what might account for it? All of these to a degree, and more.

We noted that in the former Yugoslavia ethnic conflict had first erupted in the Yugoslav Republic of Croatia in the summer of 1991. This occurred *before* Croatia's independence was actually recognised in January 1992, but at a time when it was already evident to the Croat as well as Serb inhabitants of Croatia that its independence was about to be recognised.[34] On the other hand, although there was some ethnic violence earlier, large-scale ethnic violence erupted in Bosnia-Herzegovina only *after* its independence was recognised. The eventual independence of Bosnia-Herzegovina was not certain to its population till the very last minute, since foreign governments were holding back recognition. This differentiated reaction to independence by 'minority populations' in the two republics – Croatia and Bosnia-

Herzegovina – may provide the clue to the possible roots of ethnic conflict.

The one factor that seems crucial in this context is the absence of serious ethnic conflicts while the 'international community' was believed to be committed to the 'territorial integrity' of federal Yugoslavia. Ethnic conflict erupted when it became apparent to 'minority populations' that important foreign governments were about to switch their commitment from the territorial integrity of the Yugoslavia federation to the territorial integrity of newly created *unitary* states.

As to why such a Western policy shift took place to recognition of unitary states, is not a topic for speculation here. This issue is interesting, maybe important, but not directly relevant to our concern here. The crucial fact is the formal recognition. What does concern us here is why did ethnic conflict erupt when the policy switch become apparent, in the Croatian case, or actually occurred, in the Bosnian case.

Our proposition, or hypothesis, is that the pending independence of a unitary, that is, non-federal state, is *often* perceived by its ethnically or otherwise distinct sections of a population to pose a *threat*, which they are willing to resist. That is what happened in the former Yugoslavia. Serb inhabitants perceived that as minorities in unitary states they would be repressed, become second-class citizens or, at best, would become human rights protected 'minorities'. These perceived threats they were ready to resist. The central point of our proposition is that psychological factors (perception of a threat) are primarily responsible for the eruption of conflict, not ethnic or religious differences, dislike or hostility of other groups, or the end of authoritarian rule.

Surely, not *all* diplomatic moves leading to the eruption of the violent ethnic conflicts in Bosnia-Herzegovina are known. However, the available evidence seems to show that the most significant single factor which produced that perceived threat was the recognition of its independence by the major Western governments. Lenard Cohen has noted:

> The United States' expectation that diplomatic recognition of Bosnia would calm matters seriously underestimated the history of ethnic

and religious violence in that republic, the claims to the region by Serbs and Croats, and the tenuous authority of Alija Izetbegovic's Bosnian government. The fact that Bosnia's various ethnic and religious groups had coexisted during the authoritarian Tito era, and that most inhabitants of the republic deplored ethnic rivalry, did not detract from the intense latent hatred and psychological distance existing among the various groups. Assessments of ethnic relations in Bosnia based on the cheerful atmosphere observed in Sarajevo during the 1984 Winter Olympic games, or the glib claims that the area had been an oasis of harmony for 500 years, seriously misjudged the real situation.[35]

The assessment of another observer is even more explicit:

While the West's refusal to accept Serbia's and Croatia's land grab in Bosnia is commendable, its recognition of Bosnia in April, just a month after it had proclaimed independence, will be remembered as one of the most irresponsible Western decisions in postwar history. It plunged Bosnia into the civil war.[36]

NOTES

1. Misha Glenny, *The Fall of Yugoslavia* (Penguin, 1992) p. 19.
2. L.J. Cohen, 'The Disintegration of Yugoslavia', *Current History* 91 (No. 568) (November 1992) p. 369.
3. One should add that the fascist Ustashi also killed or incarcerated in concentration camps any Jews and Gypsies they could find.
4. Serbs and Croats spoke the same language: Serbo-Croatian.
5. N.A. Stavrou, 'Unity, Brotherhood and Manipulation; Language and Minorities in Yugoslavia', *Society*, 12, 2 (Jan.–Feb., 1975), pp. 75–8.
6. Robert F. Miller, 'The Bosnian Tragedy: Historical Roots and Observations', *National Graduate*, The Australian National University (Winter 1993) p. 11.
7. Ibid., p. 12.
8. David Binder, in *The New York Times*, 1 November 1987.
9. Eric Bourne, in *The Christian Science Monitor*, 30 June 1988.
10. The autonomous republics of the Soviet Union were parts of the wide economic framework of the Soviet Union and her satellites.
11. Cohen, op. cit., p. 371.
12. For a discussion on the connection between ethnonationalism and the aspiration for statehood, see Stephanie Lawson, *The Politics of Authenticity: Ethnonationalist Conflict and the State*. Working Paper 125, Research School of Pacific Studies, The Australian National University, November 1992.

13. Cohen, op. cit., p. 372.
14. The only state in the former Yugoslavia whose citizens were not directly involved in the war is Slovenia. Whether Macedonia may be considered to be another such state is debatable.
15. R.F. Miller, 'The Dilemmas of Civil Society in Yugoslavia: The Burden of Nationalism', in R.F. Miller, ed., *The Development of Civil Society in Communist Systems* (Sydney, Australia: Allen & Unwin, 1992) p. 107.
16. Chuck Sudetic, in *The New York Times*, 16 July 1990.
17. R.F. Miller, 'The Outcomes in Former Yugoslavia', *Quadrant*, 37, 10 (October 1993) p. 64.
18. Henry Kamm, in *The New York Times*, July, 1990.
19. The Kosovo Provincial Assembly had not approved the Constitution, which abolished provincial status for Kosovo.
20. Cohen, op. cit., p. 372.
21. The subsequent chronology of events is based, in part, on reports printed in *The New York Times*. Specific attention was paid to Chuck Sudetic's 4 April 1993 piece and David Binder's 29 April 1993 piece.
22. Cohen, op. cit., p. 372.
23. *The New York Times*, 23 December 1991.
24. David Binder, in *The New York Times*, 29 August 1993.
25. Ibid.
26. Chuck Sudetic.
27. John F. Burns, in *The New York Times*, 1 May 1992.
28. The paper also reported that Major Cheko was arrested by federal Yugoslav troops in early October 1992 and jailed for his acts.
29. BBC report on 25 January 1992 of a Croatian Radio 22 January broadcast from Zagreb.
30. State Department Briefing, Federal News Service, Federal Information Systems Corporation, 14 May 1992.
31. Federal News Service, Federal Information Systems Corporation, 19 May 1992.
32. Cohen, op. cit., p. 370.
33. Dusco Duder, 'Yugoslavia: New War, Old Hatreds', *Foreign Policy*, (Summer 1993) p. 3.
34. The Croatian Assembly decided on 29 May 1991 to secede *if* certain conditions were not met; the formal declaration in Croatia and Slovenia was on 25 June 1991.
35. Cohen, op. cit., pp. 374–5.
36. Aleksa Djilas, 'The Nation that Wasn't', *The New Republic* (21 September 1992) p. 25.

Part II

In search of causes and solutions

6   Theoretical considerations

In a referendum held at the end of February 1992 on independence in Bosnia-Herzegovina, some 1.2 million Bosnian Serbs, over 30 per cent of the population, boycotted the referendum. Nevertheless, since about 60 per cent of the electorate and about 90 per cent of the participants supported that proposition, the legislative body of Bosnia-Herzegovina declared independence. Governments of Western democracies, in turn, accepted the 'will of the majority' and recognised Bosnia s independence. Our question is: Why did Bosnian Serbs not participate in the referendum, thus missing the opportunity to live in a democratic Bosnia-Herzegovina, which its government promised to create?

One possible answer to this question may be that 30 per cent of the population simply did not choose to exercise their democratic right to vote; they abstained. Another possible answer may be that Bosnian Serbs boycotted the referendum because they, as Serbs everywhere, have long been committed to the realisation of the dream of a Greater Serbia, which was to include Bosnia-Herzegovina. Still another possible answer may be that the Bosnian Serbs were merely pawns in a scheme concocted by the Belgrade government and/or the Yugoslav military and were ordered to boycott the referendum.

Even if we accept that Bosnian Serbs merely exercised their democratic right to abstain; even if the idea of a Greater Serbia was prevalent among all Serbs; even if an order to boycott the referendum was indeed issued in Belgrade – one might also consider the possibility that Bosnian Serbs boycotted the referendum because they did not like the prospect of becoming a minority in an independent Bosnia.

Long before the referendum itself, the possibility of independence was a topic of discussions not only in Belgrade but in small towns and villages of Bosnia-Herzegovina as well. There may very well have been a Belgrade plan to invade most or all of Bosnia-Herzegovina. But there is ample evidence that there were disagreements on the personal and the local levels. Many Muslim Serb mixed marriages split, neighbour rose against neighbour, Serb villagers forced Muslim villagers to flee and vice versa. Many acts of 'ethnic cleansing', that is, attempts to create ethnically 'pure' villages and regions, were personal and local initiatives. In the eyes of many Bosnian Serbs, a Muslim-dominated state, which would have been the eventual outcome of independence, appeared as a 'threat'. In this chapter we shall elaborate on the theoretical aspects of this proposition.

As preliminary steps in this elaboration we shall first discuss two topics: territoriality and democracy, and research focus.

TERRITORIALITY AND DEMOCRACY

Majority rule is an accepted practice in democratic systems. A majority vote wins – temporarily. Those who lose can try to gather a new majority in the time span between two free and fair elections. In many sovereign states, as in the United States and some other Western democracies, such a system has worked relatively well. In most democracies, those who abstain do not 'play' and are not counted either among the majority or among the minority.

At the time of the referendum in Bosnia-Herzegovina, the formerly communist Eastern European countries were already undergoing a process of democratisation which most of their citizens warmly welcomed. The support for democracy – hence majority rule – was overwhelming in the formerly communist-ruled states. Nevertheless, most Serbs in Bosnia-Herzegovina were apparently not willing to abide by the principle of majority rule. They boycotted the elections. Maybe Serbs in Bosnia-Herzegovina were not sufficiently familiar with the principle of democracy? This is an unlikely reason, for Bosnian Croats and Muslims who participated in the referendum were probably no more familiar with it than their Serb neighbours.

It is quite clear that Serbs were as familiar with democracy as were Bosnian Croats and Muslims. That is precisely the point. Bosnian Serbs were probably well aware that since they constituted only some

30 per cent of the population of Bosnia-Herzegovina, the referendum question would receive the majority of affirmative votes which would result in a Muslim-dominated government of a unitary state. Serbs probably also knew that they could have representatives in the future parliament of the independent state which, by democratic standards, should have been an acceptable outcome. By their boycott they rejected that option too.

Bosnian Serbs refused to participate in the referendum and thus rejected that democratically acceptable outcome, we propose, because they had another option which, at least in principle, was also acceptable by democratic standards. This option may be shown by a comparison between, on the one hand, the type of ethnic diversity in the United States and, on the other hand, the type of ethnic diversity in Bosnia-Herzegovina and in almost any other part of the world.

Excepting African-Americans and Native Americans, the United States is a country of immigrants. Their ethnic heritages, cultures, languages and religions are dispersed all over the country and, in many instances, blended in the American 'melting pot'. In the United States the 50 states are not aggregated around ethnic groups. Being a Californian or an Ohioan is not quite the same as being Ukrainian or Slovak in the former Soviet Union and the former Czechoslovakia respectively. In the United States the successful federal arrangement is not composed of ethnically based Mississippians and ethnically based Vermonters as constituent bodies, but rather of Americans living in Mississippi and Vermont. Ethnic diversity in the United States, excepting Native Americans and in major cities, is not territorial.

Ethnic diversity in most other parts of the world is, primarily though not exclusively, territorial. It does not mean that in every part of the world every ethnic group, everywhere, has always been territorial. Exceptions exist. For example, Armenians who lived outside the Armenian SSR or Russians who lived in the Latvian SSR were not territorial groups. However, in former Yugoslavia, and in most parts of the world, ethnic groups, nationalities, have inhabited a specific piece of land for generations. So have the Serbs. Most ethnic, national, cultural, linguistic and/or religious groups had their own historical memories connected to the lands they lived on. So have the Serbs.

While Italian-Americans and African-Americans, to use two

examples, would have difficulty opting for *territorial autonomy* instead of representation in democratic institutions, Serbs – and Croats – in Bosnia have had this option. In a state where ethnicity is territorial, such as in Croatia and in Bosnia-Herzegovina, members of each ethnic, religious, or linguistic community *might* consider themselves to be a separate 'people' or 'nation' deserving to rule themselves and not to be ruled by what they may perceive to be another 'people' or 'nation'. They might not. But, in all such cases the option does exist. Such self-perceived 'peoples' or 'nations' might develop not merely their own aggregate ideological stands and interests; they might produce their own territory-based political stands and territorially defined self-identities. Unlike in the case of dispersed ethnicity, in the case of territorial ethnicity there is the option of claiming the democratic right to self-determination, either in the form of autonomy or sovereign independence.

Territorial ethnicity need not and does not prevent intermarriages among members of different ethnic groups. Human beings from diverse cultures, ethnic or religious roots can live and have lived peacefully side by side and can interact, often despite bleak historical memories about the 'other', as have Serbs and Croats, Muslims and Christians – or Hutus and Tutsis.

In the United States, ethnic minorities are not created through elections. Elections produce a minority in the representative bodies, but neither 'minority' nor the 'majority' would represent territorial ethnic groups. The 'Black Caucus' in the United States Congress may purport to represent the interests of 'Blacks', but it does not represent, and does not purport to represent, a territorially defined group of people in the United States. Although the idea has been proposed from time to time, for the African-American 'minority' in the United States territorial autonomy or secession has not been a realistic option.

Elections in a state with territorial ethnic groups, on the other hand, can, though not always do, create a 'minority' and a 'majority' in the country, and territorial autonomy can be an option instead of or alongside representation in elected institutions. In the case of territorial ethnicity, an election or a referendum may be seen to lead not to a temporary electoral victory or defeat – which may be reversed after four or five years – but to a possibly permanent domination of 'our people' or 'our nation'. Territorial autonomy, or sovereign independence, may then be an option to avert such an eventuality.

While Bosnia-Herzegovina was part of Yugoslavia, Serbs did not consider themselves to be a 'minority' in Bosnia-Herzegovina. But many Bosnian Serbs did fear becoming a 'minority' in independent Bosnia-Herzegovina. Since many villages and regions in Bosnia-Herzegovina were inhabited primarily by Serbs, they *could* claim certain sections of Bosnia-Herzegovina as 'belonging' to them. That there was no agreement among the various parties on the size of the 'properly' Serb territory, is a separate issue.

If they had participated in the referendum, Bosnian Serbs would have been perceived as giving tacit assent to the obvious outcome of the referendum. In their eyes, they would have accepted 'minority' status in an independent Bosnia and, above all, would have been seen to have given up both the option of territorial autonomy and the option of forming part of neighbouring Serbia. Most Bosnian Serbs preferred to boycott the democratic procedure of a referendum in Bosnia-Herzegovina, for its only possible outcome, in their eyes, was the domination of their ethnic group or 'nation' by the Bosnian Muslim ethnic group or 'nation'.

RESEARCH FOCUS

Social scientists tend to take the *group* as a unit of analysis. The group may be an interest group, family, political party, trade union, or government, as well as an ethnic group, or nation. Of course, scholars do focus on the human being occasionally, such as in poll-taking before and after elections. Nonetheless, in scholarly research on ethnic conflict, the type of research which concerns us here, the unit of analysis is the ethnic group.

If one chooses to be concerned with the possible 'danger' of slipping out of the social science context, then not focusing on the group as a unit of analysis should probably be avoided. If, however, one's objective is the understanding of ethnic conflict, or any other social phenomena, whatever the proper unit of analysis may prove to be, then focus on the *human being* may appear to be a worthwhile undertaking and the presumed 'danger' irrelevant. It is proposed here that the social scientist's interdisciplinary scientific exploration of the human being, an understanding of what might be called 'human nature', is indispensable for an understanding of group behaviour, hence it should fall within the social science context.

Consider the fact, for example, that although Ustashi membership during World War II was almost exclusively Croat, not each and every adult Croat joined the Ustashi, the same as not all Serbs joined the Partisans. The historical fact is that some Serbs joined the Chetniks and some Croats joined the Ustashi's enemies – Tito's Partisans. Also, while violent ethnic conflict raged in Bosnia – when reports of 'ethnic cleansing' perpetrated by Bosnian Serbs against Muslims were circulated – some Bosnian Serbs were members of the Bosnian government. From these examples, and many others that might be quoted, it appears that not each and every Croat, Muslim, Serb – or each and every Czech, Slovak, or Magyar – has the same political stand, and self-identity, as each and every other person in the same ethnic group; nor would the behaviour of every individual be identical in the same ethnic and any other kind of group.

True, Croats, as a group – be it an ethnic group or a nation – differ in religion, alphabet and other cultural aspects, from Serbs, as a group. True also, that virtually all Serbs and Croats are different from Muslims on the basis of religion. All this however does not mean that every person in any of the three groups would always have the same views and would behave the same way as all other persons in their respective groups. The evidence is overwhelming. Many members of each of the three groups have emigrated at various periods to the United States, Australia and elsewhere. Many among them became what is called hyphenated Americans and Australians. As we noted earlier, many among the hyphenated Croat-Americans and Croat-Australians and others supported non-hyphenated Croats in Croatia in various ways while others did not.

Since members of groups do not always *behave* uniformly, studying only groups and their behaviour is not sufficient. If some members of an ethnic group engage in conflict and violent acts while others in the same ethnic group do not, we should understand why this is so. Focusing on and making general remarks about THE SERBS, THE CROATS the same as about THE JEWS, THE BLACKS is scientifically inaccurate and morally inappropriate.

In sum, focusing on the human being instead of the group does take us to a sphere of inquiry which is customarily outside the research interests of most social scientists in general and most political scientists in particular. Unfortunately, such a focus of inquiry will appear to many as diverting or irrelevant to a better understanding of the 'ethnic challenge' in Central Europe. Hopefully, for others it will prove relevant.

The reader should be forewarned that what follows is no more than a very brief summary of an approach which requires a far more detailed presentation. For the sake of brevity and readability, virtually no documentation and substantiation will be provided. Nevertheless, whatever may be the deficiencies of the presentation, its central message should not be missed. It is that without a cross-disciplinary scientific study of the human being, as such, we shall fail to understand human behaviour in general and ethnic conflict in particular. To put the argument differently and specifically: an interdisciplinary scientific exploration of the individual human being, or what might be called 'human nature', is indispensable for understanding human behaviour in general and for comprehending the factors that bring human beings to engage in ethnic conflict in particular.

THE HUMAN BEING AND TWO ENVIRONMENTS

The human body is only 'comfortable' within a limited range of *temperature*. Whatever that specific range may actually be, our bodies are surely not 'comfortable' either in a temperature of −30 degrees Fahrenheit or in a temperature of, say, +130 degrees Fahrenheit. It is also evident, to use another example, that our bodies are not 'comfortable' beyond some degree of *pain*. A light touch is fine, but a hard blow to our nose, stomach, or to virtually any part of our body causes 'discomfort', even pain. And, as a third and last example, the human body would probably be within a 'comfortable' range without *food*, or water, for a few hours, for a day, maybe two, but without food or water for several days or more our bodies would be 'uncomfortable'.[1]

All these examples refer to our bodies, to the human *physical* being. An interesting fact about these examples – and in all other

cases that may be relevant to our physical being – is that the range
between 'comfortable' and 'uncomfortable' is measurable. We *can
measure with relative ease* temperature in degrees, the intensity of a
blow to our body in lb/square inch, and count the number of days
without food or water – as well as the number of calories in food, the
number of white and red cells in our blood, and so on. Consequently,
the above-listed propositions relating to the human *physical* being
can be demonstrated and are verifiable.

Human beings also have a *psychological* (or psychic or spiritual)
range of 'comfort'. We feel 'comfortable' hearing soothing, loving,
words, and words of praise, and 'uncomfortable' when hearing their
opposites; 'comfortable' at the sight of a smiling face and
'uncomfortable' at the sight of an angry face.

However, the range of *psychological* 'comfort' and 'discomfort' is
difficult, maybe impossible, to measure. It is difficult to measure a
'comfortable' or 'uncomfortable' sight (reaching our brains through
our eyes), a 'comfortable' or an 'uncomfortable' *sound* (reaching our
brains through our ears). Because of the difficulty – or the impos-
sibility – of measuring psychological 'comfort' and 'discomfort', it is
difficult to prove that such ranges exist and it is therefore easy to
dismiss propositions about them. For the same reason, one may
readily argue, actually to hold on to the widely held belief that each
human being has his or her own personal preferences of psychological
'comfort' and 'discomfort'. Our proposition is that it is not the case.

True, personal differences do exist *within* the psychological range.
But that is also true within the physical range. Some human beings
can better tolerate than others higher temperatures and heavier
blows, as well as 'uncomfortable' sights, sounds. There are also
human beings – religious devotees, maybe others – who can reach
beyond the range. However, such exceptions and personal differences
do not negate the existence of a range of 'comfort' and 'discomfort' in
both physical and psychological categories.

The examples about *psychological* 'comfort' and 'discomfort'
included sounds of *words* (such as in a language) and sights (such as
the colour or shape) of *faces*. Now, a composite of 'comfortable'
words and sights – possibly along with a few other factors – may
produce what one might call 'love' toward parents, siblings, friends,
spouses or other human beings. A composite of a different set of

'comfortable' words and sights – possibly along with other factors – may produce 'trust', 'sense of freedom', 'safety', and so on. Inversely, a composite of 'uncomfortable' words and sights – possibly along with other factors – may produce what one might call 'hate', and a composite of a different set of 'uncomfortable' words and sights – possibly along with other factors – may produce 'mistrust', a sense of 'unfreedom', 'threat', and so on.

The examples about physical 'comfort' and 'discomfort' included temperature (that clothes and shelter provide), touch, and food. Now, a composite of 'comfortable' temperature and touch – possibly along with a few other factors – may produce what one might call 'health'. A composite of a different set of 'comfortable' tangibles – such as food and water – may produce 'well-being', 'a full stomach', and so on. Inversely, a composite of 'uncomfortable' temperature and touch – possibly along with other factors – may produce what one might call 'illness', and a composite of a different set of 'uncomfortable' tangibles may produce 'hunger', 'thirst', and so on.

Here are then our propositions:

(1) Human beings feel 'comfortable' interacting with human beings in a socio-political environment which provides *psychological* 'comfort', and feel 'uncomfortable' interacting with human beings in a socio-political environment which produces *psychological* 'discomfort'. Consequently, there is a human tendency to stay within or to seek out psychologically – socio-politically – 'comfortable' environments.

(2) Human beings feel 'comfortable' in a physical – economic – environment which provides *physical* 'comfort', and feel 'uncomfortable' in a physical environment which *produces* conditions of physical 'discomfort'. Consequently, there is a human tendency to stay within or to seek out physically – economically – 'comfortable' environments.

HUMAN BEINGS – HUMAN NEEDS

In order to be in the range of *physical* 'comfort', human beings *need*, first and foremost, nutritious food and shelter from extreme cold and heat. In order to be in the range of *psychological* 'comfort', human beings *need*, among others, love, sense of belonging, respect, a sense of freedom, a sense of pride and self-esteem.

The word 'need' and the phrase 'human needs' are part of everyday vocabulary. The pharase is often used in the context of economic development.[2] In its everyday usage, 'human needs' is usually not related to the special meaning we shall attach to the phrase.

'Human needs' as we use it, pertains to the requirements of the human being, as a human organism, for physical and psychological (or psychic) survival and, by extension, well-being. Physical survival means staying physically alive and healthy; psychological survival means staying psychologically alive and healthy. 'Well-being' pertains to a condition beyond survival and health and connotes a 'decent' living standard.

Human needs are not acquired or learned habits; they are 'dictated' by the human organism. In other words, the needs, for example, for food and love, are not learned habits but the requirements of the human body and psyche respectively. Food is a human need not because it is customary to eat food, or because one thinks that eating is a good idea, but because the human *organism* needs food. Food, and every other human need is anchored in a potentiality of the human organism. Love, being loved, is a human need not because loving and being loved are a good idea, but because the human *organism* needs love. A newborn baby, a biological organism, has the *potentiality* to become an adult human being and to *survive* within a certain range of 'comfortable' environments and conditions. However, both the newborn baby and the adult human being *need* food and love, to use two examples, for survival and – by extension – well-being.

The two main categories of needs are 'physical needs' and 'psychic, or psychological, needs'. Each of these main categories of needs is composed of a long list of specific needs, some of which tend to and often do overlap. In the set of the *physical* needs of the human organism one might list, among others, food, water, shelter (for the avoidance of extreme cold and heat), touch, and sex (not love). In the set of *psychic* needs one might list, among others, love, respect, appreciation, friendship, and a sense of belonging, as well as the *sense of being free from the opposites* of all the above, such as hatred, disrespect, lack of appreciation, and alienation. Among the psychic needs we may also include intellectual and religious needs. Again, the specific needs tend to overlap and they do overlap, especially in the set of psychological needs, where no specific element is easily measurable nor indeed precisely definable. Here is a summary of some of our propositions:

(1) Each human being is an organism with two *sets* of needs.
(2) Each human being, their organism, is 'driven' by the potentiality imbedded in the human organism to satisfy *both* sets of needs.
(3) The 'drive' for the satisfaction of *physical needs* aims at physical survival (and well-being), which may be attained in favourable *economic* environments and conditions.
(4) The 'drive' and aspiration for the satisfaction of *psychological needs* aims at psychological survival (and well-being), which may be attained in favourable *socio-political* environments and conditions.

In sum, the set of physical needs includes the well-being of the human *body*; the set of psychic needs includes the well-being of what we might call the human *spirit*.

'FEATURES' AND 'IDENTITIES'

Both sets of needs are *personal* needs. Each human being, as a separate organism, feels hungry or not being loved. Each and every one of the five or six billion human beings that make up humanity has 'needs' of a certain number of calorie intake, and 'needs' for an unmeasurable degree of 'freedom'. Each human being has his or her own biological and nervous system, and satisfaction of needs or lack of them is, in this sense, personal.

Human beings are social animals. That basically means that human beings must interact with each other in order to satisfy their psychological needs. Human beings are also economic animals. This basically means that human beings must interact with the physical environment and with other human beings in order to satisfy their physical needs.

As long as both sets of needs of a human being are *perceived* by that human being to be satisfied, he or she will peacefully interact with other human beings and with the physical environment. If, however, either or both sets of needs are *perceived* to be unsatisfied, or about not to be satisfied, then peaceful interaction might turn to either relocation, emigration or conflict.

If and when *physical* needs are seen not to be satisfied, or about not to be satisfied which, in modern times, may be due to unemployment, a human being might relocate to a region where such needs may be satisfied. Thus, citizens of the United States moved, say, from the south to find employment in California, and Yugoslav citizens moved in the 1960s and 1970s to work in western Europe. There are other human beings who emigrate – for economic reasons – from one country to another. Relocation or emigration may occur also if psychic needs are perceived not to be satisfied. Citizens in the United States have moved from towns to rural areas in search of safety and tranquillity; many Croats left communist-ruled Yugoslavia for democratic countries.

If, however, the human being perceiving either or both sets of needs not to be satisfied does *not* relocate or emigrate – often as a refugee – then a conflict situation might emerge. This is the focus of our interest here. Here is our first hypothesis in this regard:

> Only those human beings are likely to enter into relations
> of conflict who *perceive*, at a given time, a threat to satisfac-
> tion of one or more components in either or both of their
> two sets of needs.

Let us note here two aspects of this hypothesis. First, conflict erupts in case of perceived unsatisfied needs. The second, which we shall examine now, is that a transformation occurs from peaceful interaction to conflict relations.

What happens when human beings who have interacted peacefully with other human beings, as they did for over 40 years in Yugoslavia? This question brings us to the important distinction between 'features' and 'identities'.

'Features' is a label for a long list of human characteristics which may include, among many others: tall, skinny, white, good dancer, polite, having curly hair, and so on. 'Features' are dominant in peaceful interactions among human beings, in any non-conflict situation. To put it differently, peaceful or cooperative interaction among human beings will last as long as differences among human beings remain 'features'.

'Identity' in turn is an *emphasised* 'feature'. In other words, a 'feature', such as skinny – if emphasised, if picked out – will turn to be an identity. That transformation from 'feature' to 'identity' we call activation of identity.

Identities are activated in a variety of circumstances. For example, a person in the United States from an African country, who on the basis of his or her *features* may appear to be African-American, may *identify* himself or herself and say: 'I am not an African-American, I am African; more specifically I am from Ghana.' Similarly, a white American tourist in Europe might specify that he or she is not English but an American. In both cases a personal identity was activated. In both cases conflict situations are unlikely to emerge. Activation of a personal identity does not necessarily lead to conflict.

Often, a large number of human beings activate a shared identity and thus a group identity emerges. Here then is our proposition:

> Human beings activate a shared identity, and thus form a group of 'us' in order to attain more effectively than any of them could alone the satisfaction of their human needs.

Activation of personal identity is typical *not* in western cultural settings, but in settings where economic, political or social *competition* is prevalent. Thus, introduction of capitalist competition into non-western cultural settings will stimulate activation of personal identities. Similarly, activation of group identity is typical *not* in non-western settings, but in settings where the group identity appears more effective for satisfying human needs. We have seen in recent years that activation of an ethnic or religious identity is as likely to occur in Europe as in other parts of the world. Above all, what we have been calling group identity in the non-western world are not identities at all but shared 'features'.

In sum, we propose that the word 'identity' should be applied to specific phenomena and not used in an unrestricted way as we do in everyday speech. The one possible way we could arrive at such a specificity is by using two different labels for different manifestations of the same phenomenon. One label would be 'identity', the other 'features'.

ACTIVATION OF IDENTITY AND CONFLICT

Elections, referenda, or declarations of war, are among the factors that may bring about the *activation* of an identity, but not necessarily by everyone.

While some Serbs, as noted earlier, participated in 'ethnic cleansing', other Serbs were members of the government of Bosnia-Herzegovina. While many Croats were members of the Ustashi during World War II and were deeply involved in atrocities, other Croats were neither its members nor participated in those acts. Thus, it would be inaccurate to say that the *Croats* – having their shared 'features' – and the *Serbs* – having their shared 'features' – entered in relations of conflict. It would be more accurate to say that *some* Croats and Serbs activated their Croat or Serb identity, while others did not. Moreover, those human beings who activated their identities and entered in relations of conflict at one time, may have lived in relative peace, and even cooperated with their present enemies at an earlier time. Such oscillation between 'feature' and 'identity', between cooperation and conflict, has occurred in the ethnically heterogeneous former Yugoslavia – and Bosnia-Herzegovina – where decades passed without violent ethnic conflict.

Since ethnic conflict neither engages *everyone* on either side, nor engages individual human beings all the time, it follows that conflict, ethnic or otherwise, is not caused by existing differences between ethnic groups – whether based on language, culture, religion or historical memories – since such differences exist at all times – during both peaceful and conflict relations – and are inevitably noticed, on both sides, by all members of an ethnic group.

Why and when do some human beings enter in relations of conflict while others, members of the same ethnic group, do not?

If *each* human being has these two sets of needs which they are *always* 'driven' to satisfy, and if only *some* human beings are in relations of conflict – and only some of the time, even though ethnic differences exist all the time – then a correlation may exist between a person's sense of unsatisfied needs at a given time and his or her participation in conflict at that time.

The activation of a shared identity is a complex process. For the activation to occur, human beings must first be conscious of their moral and legal right to the satisfaction of their two sets of needs. We may call these rights 'moral principles'. There must be an actual or aspiring 'political entrepreneur' who conveys that right; *conditions* that are seen to pose a threat to the satisfaction of the two sets of needs; an *obstacle*, another group, against whom an identity is activated and conflict ensues. The following complex sentence summarises this process:

> Conflict occurs when a *political entrepreneur* conveying the *'moral principles'* to *human beings* and convincing them to *perceive* negatively either their *political or their economic conditions or both*, succeeds in *activating a shared identity* in a *polarised* opposition to an *obstacle*, which may be the *government* or other group of human beings, in order to reach their *target of aspirations*.

It should be added, that while negatively perceived *economic* conditions produce a perceived threat to *physical* needs, hence to *physical* survival and well-being; negatively perceived *socio-political* conditions entail a threat to *psychic* (or psychological) needs, hence to *psychic* (or psychological) survival and well-being.

All these observations or premises may be summarised in the following hypothesis:

> Human behaviour is the by-product of the personal human 'drive' to satisfy two sets of human needs, physical needs and psychic (psychological) needs – and to avoid prospects for non-satisfaction of either or both needs.

Participation in ethnic conflict is a form of human behaviour. Participation in an ethnic (or other type of) conflict is one possible response to a perceived threat to the satisfaction of either one or both sets of human needs. Joining the government and emigrating, to use two other examples, may be different responses to the same. Thus, a perceived threat to 'human needs' may be at the root of ethnic conflict, as well as other forms of human behaviour.

ETHNIC GROUP AND IDENTITY

Marx's thesis that class identity is the true identity, may have been wrong. But, it does not mean that ethnic or national *identities* are the 'true' identities in any meaningful sense of the word.

What is generally referred to as 'ethnic' identity is one of a range of possible identities that human beings might activate. Other identities that may be activated revolve around economic status, and/or gender, education, skin colour, ideology, marital status, disability, profession, membership in 'the colonised', and so on. What is so special about ethnic identity?

The features which are usually taken as components of an ethnic identity – mother tongue, culture, religion, historical memories – are easy to activate, for they are ever-present. The activation of these identities can form the largest groups of 'us'; they serve as the most clearly distinguishable differences among human beings and between two or more groups of human beings. Ethnic identities can be activated in modern societies as well as in 'pre-modern' ones; by the educated as well as by the uneducated. In sum, activation of *ethnic* identities is frequent, for they are universally available, widely shared and easily distinguishable by the participants.

The activation of class identity in nineteenth-century Germany – and elsewhere – may have been less frequent and intense hence less 'successful' than activation of national identity, at least in part, because it has been easier to mobilise human beings by bringing them to activate their *ethnic/national* identities, than by bringing them to activate their *proletarian* identity.

Ethnic groups, or 'nations', are not organic entities. The organic entity is the human being, *defined* by its two sets of needs. Ethnic and 'national' identities are produced by the activation of shared identities in order to satisfy personal human needs. Without an activation of a shared identity there is no group self-identity; without the activation of an ethnic identity there is no ethnic conflict.

If so, at the core of 'nationalism', ethnic or otherwise, is not an abstract idea, creed, or ideology. At its core are the needs of the human organism. More specifically, ethnic conflict, and some forms of nationalism within sovereign states (nationalism 'from below'), are anchored in a perceived *threat* to either physical or psychic needs and well-being. The motor of change in post-French Revolutionary history, in nineteenth-century Europe, and in contemporary Central Europe is not 'nationalism' but the spreading message that human beings have the *right* – are entitled – to satisfy both sets of human needs. If that is so, then the satisfaction of the two sets of human needs may present the very elusive 'resolution' of conflict which social scientists have long pursued.

ETHNIC CONFLICT AND THE STATE

Satisfying *psychological* needs of human beings in ethnically diverse modern sovereign states is a challenging task. Where such a challenge is not fully met, ethnic identities may be readily activated. In such states, any 'political entrepreneur' has a relatively easy task of mobilising human beings against 'others', portrayed as the 'obstacle'. If ethnicity is territorial, autonomy may also be claimed.

Furthermore, activation of ethnic identities in ethnically diverse sovereign states can more easily occur if its government is democratic. The right to organise political parties in preparation for free and fair elections provides unhindered opportunity for new 'political entrepreneurs' to mobilise followers activating their ethnic identities. This has occurred in post-communist states of Central and Eastern Europe.

Of course, democratic institutions, such as representative bodies and free and fair elections, are institutional means to satisfy the need for 'freedom', a sense of belonging, possibly pride. However, democratic institutions are merely means through which 'freedom' is to be provided. Democratic institutions may also actually produce restrictions on 'freedom' – such as in Nazi Germany – or be perceived to produce restrictions on 'freedom' – at a given moment or in the future. In such cases identities may be activated in search for other means to 'freedom'. If a territorial ethnic identity is activated and a self-identified ethnic group emerges, then that ethnic group might demand the *democratic right to self-rule* as a more effective means to achieve 'freedom'.

Satisfying *physical* needs within a state is also a challenging task. The task is even more challenging in those sovereign states where material and/or human resources are scarce and where obtaining sufficient amounts of needed resources through import-export, foreign investment, or foreign aid is problematic. It may be that 'free market' institutions and processes are more instrumental to satisfy physical needs than state-controlled institutions and practices. However, although substitution of one set of *means* by another may create the initial expectation and anticipation, 'free-market' institutions and processes are not *in themselves* adequate to satisfy the physical needs for survival, let alone the growing personal aspiration for economic well-being, that is, a decent standard of living. Furthermore, human beings in the post-Cold War era are no longer likely to accept merely equal *opportunities* to obtain resources for their economic well-being. Thus, an ideological commitment to a specific *means* used or proposed for the improvement of economic conditions, be it socialism or capitalism, lasts only and as long as the means, that is, the institutions, are perceived to *provide*, or perceived to lead *soon*, to what each human organism is 'driven' towards – physical survival and economic well-being through the satisfaction to physical needs.

If ethnic conflict is a by-product of unsatisfied needs, then to prevent, reduce, or eliminate ethnic conflict the two sets of needs must be satisfied.

Satisfying *psychological* needs of human beings in states where ethnicity is diverse and territorial, and satisfying physical needs in states where resources are limited are difficult tasks which probably cannot be met by the preferred means of democracy and private enterprise alone. If democratisation will not bring about the satisfaction of relevant psychic needs, and privatisation will not bring about the satisfaction of relevant physical needs in the ethnically diverse countries of post-Cold War Central Europe, then the potential of ethnic conflict will continue to exist. Successful response to the human 'drive to satisfy both sets of human needs may require not merely *regime transformation* within sovereign states –

from totalitarianism to democracy, from state control of the economy to privatisation – but also *structural transformation* of those sovereign states.

This proposition may be restated in a motto:

> If you wish to prevent, reduce, or end ethnic conflict, ask not how to fit human beings into the framework of sovereign state (be it Bosnia-Herzegovina or any other); ask what kind of political and economic frameworks might fit human beings (be they Serbs or any others).

ETHNIC CONFLICT AND STRUCTURAL CHANGE

Perceived *threat* to the satisfaction of *psychic needs* opens the road to the activation of a shared ethnic identity and to conflict. In a state with territorial ethnicity, which Bosnia-Herzegovina is to become, those human beings who activated their ethnic identities in the past will *tend* to aim at the creation of a 'comfortable' socio-political entity in the future. A 'comfortable' socio-political entity is one that caters to the satisfaction of psychological needs. Such a socio-political framework will tend to be ethnically homogeneous and relatively small. We may call this gravitation toward the psychologically 'comfortable' socio-political entity – the *centripetal* trend. Bosnian Serbs have been participants in this trend.

Perceived *threat* to the satisfaction of *physical needs* also opens the road to the activation of the same shared ethnic identity, and to propel human beings toward a 'comfortable' economic framework. The 'comfortable' framework, the one likely to cater to physical needs, would be an economic framework that tends to be diverse in resources, relatively large, rich in quantity, quality and types of resources. We call this gravitation toward the physically 'comfortable' economic framework – the *centrifugal* trend.[3] Bosnian Serbs, had they gained the 'comfortable' socio-political entity, would have been participants in this trend as well.

The centripetal *trend* within a sovereign state, prompted by a perceived threat, does impinge on the *political* sovereignty of that state; the centrifugal *trend* does impinge on the *economic* sovereignty of that state. Thus, frustrated aspirations for the satisfaction of human needs *propel* toward a split between political and economic sovereignties which, through the so-called 'evolution' of the state, became vested – and then trapped – in the modern, sovereign, nation-state.[4]

The two trends – the centrifugal and the centripetal – do not counter but rather complement each other: the more small, ethnically self-defined, socio-politically autonomous, even politically sovereign, entities emerge, the more compelling it will be for members of those small, ethnically self-defined, entities to attach themselves to, maybe to be confederal components of, a wider economic framework than the state to which they now belong, or the one to which they are slated to belong.[5]

All this basically means is that both the centrifugal and centripetal trends are propelled by unsatisfied human needs.

During the 40-year-long Cold War confrontation, the centrifugal and centripetal trends were restrained, constrained, or re-channelled. With the end of the Cold War, restrains and constraints have weakened, if not totally disappeared. As a result, frustrated aspirations for freedom from communist, Russian, and Serb rule have already broken down old frameworks in the former Soviet Union and Yugoslavia. These were part of the centripetal trend. So has been the fight of Serbs for autonomy in Croatia and Bosnia-Herzegovina.

*

The problem we are facing today in the former Yugoslavia and elsewhere is not ethnic conflict *per se*: ethnic conflict is merely one symptom of the problem. The problem we are facing is how to satisfy the two sets of human needs. Our central proposition is that ethnic conflict will revert to peaceful human interactions if ethnic *identity* ceases to be activated. Ethnic identity can be deactivated, if the perceived threat to either or both sets of needs is eliminated. That, in turn, may be attained through structural change. Without structural change, at least the potential for ethnic conflict will continue to exist.

Any conflict, including ethnic conflict, can reach the degree of violence reached in Yugoslavia. For it is not the 'nature' of one of the parties involved – their 'primitiveness', 'savagery', social status, level of education, historical memories, or degree of hatred – that leads to violent acts against an 'other', but the intensity of the *perceived threat* to the satisfaction of either or both sets of their human needs.

These propositions should be closely examined and must be tested. Here they are merely propositions, or hypotheses. However, there is no clear-cut empirical evidence that the arguments that our propositions seek to reject are valid. There is no clear-cut evidence that ethnic differences *cause* ethnic conflict. The evidence seems to show that ethnic diversity *can* remain politically irrelevant for long periods, or at least politically irrelevant *enough* not to bring about violent conflict. In order for conflict to erupt 'something' must intervene and prompt a transformation from 'features' to 'identities', the *activation of politically relevant ethnic identities*. It is unfortunate and disturbing that such a 'something' may include, for example, the introduction of free competition for political power.

The possible remedy is *not* the banning of free competition for political power, a core element in democracy. If the aim is prevention and reduction of ethnic conflict, one should not be exclusively concerned with democratisation, economic reforms, protection of human rights and providing merely cultural autonomy to 'minorities' *within* sovereign states. One should *also* devote time to the exploration of possible structural changes of sovereign states.

A fairly common scholarly view is that ethnic conflict originates in awakened pre-modern sentiments, which are used in a struggle for the creation of nation-states, modern homes for the ethnic groups concerned. Stephanie Lawson has written, for example: 'Ethnicity is thus invested with the requisite moral-cultural element in terms of which the rectification of past injustice entails the establishment of a sovereign state for the group in question ...'[6] She added: 'The normative assumption that we *should* live in a world of authentic nation-states is at the very centre of ethnonationalist logic.'[7]

The only correction we propose is that 'the normative assumption' at the centre of 'ethnonationalist logic' may be not 'that we should live in a world of authentic nation-states', but that '*we should live*' in *any* structural arrangement which may provide self-rule to self-identified, territorial ethnic groups. That structural arrangement may also include territorial autonomy or various versions of a confederal arrangement.

Marx argued that the proletariat is the true revolutionary force. It has long been obvious to many that he was wrong. But wrong also are those who maintain that the true revolutionary force is the ethnic group or nation. We have proposed that the true revolutionary force is the *human being*. It is the human being who is engaged in a revolution against perceived unfreedom and unsatisfied economic needs.

Marx was surely wrong in believing that proletarian revolutions would bring about the 'withering away' of the state. But Western thinkers were also wrong to assume that the nation-state would for-ever serve as the best framework in which to prevent the Hobbesian war of all against all. Here we suggest that there is a trend toward the 'withering away' of the state – as we know it. For, as more and more human beings become aware of their human *rights* to satisfy their needs, the more and more will human beings be likely to perceive a threat to the satisfaction of their two sets of needs and push for structural change of the state. The human being does not participate in the revolution because he or she is a member of the proletariat, of a nation, of an ethnic group; but because he or she is a human being. Not ideology, but the human organism is the instigator of that revolution. And Marxism notwithstanding, the human being will rebel against all perceived domination and oppression, be it cultural, racial, religious, ethnic, gender, regional or economic.

Since ethnic conflicts of the future, ethnic revolutions, are likely to be violent – including 'ethnic cleansing' – we should choose not to wait until conditions ripen in each state for ethnic conflicts and nationalist manifestations to burst out in full force. In this post-Cold War era we might possibly assist the centrifugal and centripetal forces to bring about the erection of new *structures* in which the two sets of needs of all human beings may be better satisfied.

NOTES

1. 'Comfortable' and 'uncomfortable' are not very specific terms and may not be well chosen. Further below the phrases 'favourable' and 'unfavourable' condi-tions will also be used. These are not very telling either. Nevertheless, for lack of better choice of words at the moment, and in order to avoid confusion, 'comfortable' and 'favourable' will be used synonymously, with 'uncomfortable' and 'unfavourable' as their synonymous opposites.

2. See, for example, 'Declaration on the Establishment of a New International Economic Order', *General Assembly Resolution* 3201 (S-VI), 1 May 1974. See also: *The Planetary Bargain: Proposals for a New International Economic Order to Meet Human Needs: A Consensus Statement by the Aspen Institute International Workshop* (Princeton, NJ: Aspen Institute for Humanistic Studies, Program in International Affairs, 1975); and John McHale and Magda McHale, *Basic Human Needs: A Framework for Action* (New Brunswick, NJ: Transaction Books, 1978).

3. There is disagreement about the respective direction of the two forces. Centrifugal, according to the dictionary, means moving or tending to move away from a centre; centripetal, means moving or tending to move toward a centre. I can be easily persuaded to change the labels; the important point for the thesis is that the two forces tend to move in opposite directions.

4. It should be emphasised that we do *not* propose to erect ethnically homogeneous entities, nor do we *propose* splitting the sovereign state. We merely suggest, on the basis of our analysis, that such *trends* actually exist.

5. Inversely, the wider the economic framework – that is, the greater the prospects of access to more and varied resources – the greater will likely be the desire, indeed the possibility, to create small, self-defined, socio-politically autonomous entities *within* that wider economic framework.

6. Stephanie Lawson, 'The Politics of Authenticity: Ethnonationalist Conflict and the State', *Working Paper 125*, Peace Research Centre, Research School of Pacific Studies, The Australian National University (November 1992), p. 24.

7. Lawson, op. cit., p. 28.

7   Policy recommendations

In the previous chapter, 'Theoretical considerations', we focused on the human being as a unit of analysis and proposed that satisfying the two sets of human needs, the key to reduction of ethnic conflict, requires structural change. We also proposed that the *long evolving* structural change is propelled by complementary centrifugal and centripetal forces, themselves anchored in the human organism. In this chapter, 'Policy recommendations', we shall propose institutional arrangements that might assist the ongoing trend.

Transforming our 'theoretical considerations' into 'policy recommendations' is a difficult undertaking. Even if our 'theoretical considerations' are found by some scholars and policy makers 'challenging' or even 'worthy of close examination', their representation in policy terms could still be deemed 'impractical' and 'unrealistic', primarily because governments would not be inclined to implement them.

In response to such criticism we reply, first, that the structural change has already been taking place and we shall try to bring further evidence to that effect. In other words, we do not propose a new structural change but merely try to draw attention to it, explain its meaning and suggest measures to enhance it. Second, governments tend to be replaced by new ones under democratic regimes, and rejection of a policy by today's government may turn to be acceptance by a new one. As examples, we might mention the changing policies of the British government regarding membership in the European Community and, closer to our focus, the change of policies toward 'minorities' from the first post-communist government of Hungary to the second elected government. Third, change of ideas and circumstances is constant and what appears objectionable policy at a certain time may appear to be acceptable at a future time. One might take as a relevant example the changing policies and attitudes in Central European countries toward the Romani people, including accepting the changing of their name from Gypsy to Romani.

An ambivalent reaction to our policy recommendations, on the other hand, is understandable. The present post-Cold War era is turbulent, too complex in comparison with the bipolar world that preceded it, and the structures that we claim are now evolving have probably no historical precedents by which they could be evaluated. It is understandable therefore that many scholars and political practitioners tend to assess ongoing and future structural changes from long-established or at least long-debated perspectives. Consequently, we prefer to present our policy recommendations, not for implementation but only for consideration and debate both among scholars and policy makers.

In order to enhance the possibility that such debate might indeed take place we shall try, first, to contrast our propositions with what we believe to be a widely held view of the origins of ethnic conflict and ways to reduce ethnic conflict.

A considerably simplified presentation of the widely held view of the origins of ethnic conflict may be as follows: the jury is still out debating the issue. Among the arguments is that ethnic conflict erupts when more or less dormant hostilities among ethnic groups are awakened. Another and related argument is that ethnic groups have various interests, and ethnic conflict is a confrontation between or among the interests and – one might add – it is a struggle for power. In order to resolve conflict, members of the groups in conflict should be brought together to air their views; they should try to find a compromise between their conflicting interests, which should be sought, and, overall, the value of democratic processes inculcated and democracy consolidated. Among additional ways of resolutions offered are cooptation of ethnic leaders into existing non-ethnic political parties, thus creating 'balanced tickets'; introduction of various corporatist devices and other mechanisms of 'elite management'; and institutionalisation of various forms of ethnic spoils systems, such as affirmative action.[1] It may be appropriate to note here that these propositions share certain common denominators. They focus on a group as such, take 'interest' and struggle for power as leading factors in conflict, suggest working with leaders, elites, of such groups and, above all, they hold that resolution of the ethnic conflict is to be attained, one way or another, *within the framework of the democratic sovereign state*.

We, in turn, propose the following:

> Human beings do have interests and ethnic groups may have shared interests, but human beings also have needs, which are more fundamental and constant than interests. Dormant hostilities are not the *causes* of conflict but *instruments* in conflict. Ethnic conflicts have their origins in unsatisfied human needs. Ethnic groups fight for power but, often, they fight for power in order to be able to resist others having power over them. Human beings – alone and in groups having a shared identity – fight against being ruled by a perceived 'other', they fight for self-rule. Ethnic leaders, elites, may be coopted one way or another; however, if needs of human beings are not satisfied, new leaders – or, as we called them, political entrepreneurs – are likely to emerge again and again.
>
> In order to resolve conflict, primary attention should be directed toward the satisfaction of the two sets of human needs. The two kinds of human needs require two completely different sets of mechanisms to satisfy them, hence they require two different kinds of frameworks (see Chapter 6).

These propositions also share certain common denominators. They focus on the human being as such, take 'human needs' as a leading factor in conflict, and consider working with elites unrewarding, at least in the long run.

We might also add, that the number of human beings aware of their rights is growing and demands for the satisfaction of their needs without delay intensifying. It will become increasingly difficult to satisfy human needs within the single framework of the nation-state. Since the now evolving structural change leads, in our view, toward more effective satisfaction of human needs and reduction of ethnic conflict, it deserves to be assisted.

Let us contrast certain aspects of these two perspectives and further clarify our theoretical argument in reference to historical data.

STRUCTURAL CHANGE AND THE STATE

A widely held scholarly opinion is that the 'state', the 'nation-state', has *evolved* over the centuries. There is sufficient historical evidence to show this observation to be correct if, but only if, the word 'evolution' is taken to refer to changing relations, institutions and practices. Relations between landowners and peasants, for example, have evolved over the centuries, so have representative institutions and political participation. However, the *framework* within which this evolution has taken place, the boundaries of states, have rarely, if ever, evolved, but have been created and recreated through inter-marriages among monarchs, wars, treaties, colonial expansion, and so on. The various types of state frameworks – nation-states, empires, kingdoms – were 'artificial' creations. The existence of artificial – and subsequently 'necessary', 'legitimate' and 'inviolable' – frame-works have, in turn, affected the evolution of relations, institutions and practices within the state.

During the past 200 years of Central European history, the terri-tories of states were carved up in secret meetings and conferences which were held before and during the Congress of Vienna, 1814–15 and, in general, prior to the establishment of the Dual Monarchy in 1867. Secret meetings and conferences for the same purpose were also held during and after World War I and produced, among others, a truncated Hungary and the sovereign states of Czechoslovakia and Yugoslavia. 'Minorities' – members of ethnic groups or nationalities – were to accommodate themselves within the newly drawn boundaries the best they could, with or without the assistance of evolving institutions. That means, in terms of the terminology introduced in Chapter 6, that human beings tried to satisfy their two sets of needs within the artificial boundaries of sovereign states. Many attempts eventually failed, and many of the ethnically diverse sovereign states became fertile grounds for ethnic conflicts.

Other states in Central Europe, and states in other regions of the world, were not the products of artificial map-making by statesmen, but either the by-products of wars, dynastic marriages, colonisation, or other historic happenstance. Thus, in western Europe, Great Britain, as a state framework, has come to include the Irish, Welsh and the Scots; France, to include Bretons, Corsicans, Alsatians, Occitanians; Spain to include Basques and Catalans; Belgium to include Flamands and Walloons, to mention only a few examples.

The widely held public and scholarly view is that except for the Irish in Great Britain, other 'minorities' in western European states did successfully accommodate themselves through their evolving 'national' institutions and practices. The western European democratic states, the argument goes, are by and large the models of successful integration. Perhaps so in comparison with other parts of the world. But, even if we overlook or dismiss as insignificant the demands by Basques, or the rather tenuous ethnic relations in Belgium and elsewhere, do we really have sufficient historical perspective to judge? Besides, all the above listed states – Great Britain, France, Spain and Belgium – are today members of the European Union. May it be that 'minorities' have been successfully 'integrated' not so much into their respective sovereign 'nation-states' – or not so much through their evolved *national* institutions – but into the European Community (Union) and through *its* evolving institutions. In any case, the European Union has already perforated the boundaries of member states and diffused to some degree the political powers of their institutions.

How about other parts of the world? Need it be mentioned again that most states in Africa and many in Asia have inherited colonial boundaries – without the slightest consideration for their human composition let alone their economic viability – as well as western institutions and practices. In many of them ethnic conflicts are rampant, while in many others tentatively contained.

How about states in which ethnic conflicts are rare or non-existent? Australia is an island-state where Native Australians have been demanding rights relatively quietly; within the boundaries of the United States only the different Native American groups form territorial ethnicities; Japan is ethnically almost homogeneous; and, in the artificially created Latin American states, 'minorities', ethnic groups or 'nations', have just begun to awaken to their rights. The effectiveness of their evolved western institutions, even if and where they could be considered institutionalised, are hardly tested.

We might say, in reference to the end of the previous chapter, that throughout history, minorities, ethnic groups, or nations – in fact human beings – were to 'fit themselves' or were to be 'fitted' – to the artificially created state. It has been so since the emergence of ancient Egypt some five thousand years ago – arguably the first known political entity in history – to the independence of Bosnia-Herzegovina less than three years ago. In the distant past, as now, the main concern of rulers of all types has been the maintenance of internal stability and safeguarding the territorial integrity of states which, in modern times, have also become the indispensable components of the international system.

Much has changed of course since the emergence of ancient Egypt. But a closer look would show that some of these changes over the millennia were cosmetic rather than substantive. May we be permitted the rather cynical remark, that in ancient Egypt god-kings coordinated the 'fitting', later absolute monarchs, later anointed as representatives of the one God; while in modern times, a mythical 'people', or one 'nation' – in fact often an amalgam of ethnies and nations – substituted for god as the sovereign source of power and authority, to carry out the task of 'fitting'.

The methods rulers and governments used over the centuries have also varied from the very harsh to the tolerant. Nevertheless, internal and international policies and actions – and contemporary scholarly approaches – may be classified into two analytically distinguishable but often alternatively used and overlapping categories. One category includes the morally repulsive and by human rights standards unacceptable responses to challenges posed by ethnic demands. They include expulsion, extermination, forced religious conversion, forced assimilation, banishment, and various forms of discrimination. In the second category are included the morally acceptable responses by human rights standards, such as the right to vote and to representation, the granting of language, cultural, civil, and human rights, linguistic and cultural autonomy, protection of minorities, and various other measures introduced by evolved democratic institutions.

One of the tragedies of social life is that the morally *unacceptable* measures are more effective than the morally acceptable ones. Among the morally *acceptable* responses some have been effective some of the time. However, the outbreak of the two world wars is itself at least partial proof for the overall failure of morally acceptable measures. In the post-Cold War era, the intended and already introduced morally acceptable responses of governments and international organisations were not essentially different from those proposed in and since the nineteenth century. The outbreak of violent conflict in Yugoslavia is at least a partial proof of *their repeated* failure.

Many morally acceptable attempts failed to reduce, let alone prevent, ethnic conflict because they have been implemented in reverse order. First the right to self-determination was accorded to expediently, and artificially created *states*; then, not self-determination, but 'minority rights' and internationally guaranteed 'human rights' and other morally acceptable responses were introduced to serve as remedies for the 'ethnic' or 'national' discontent that the creation of the new state produced. This reverse order is what we have called fitting human beings to the state.

The artificially created states patterned, at best, on nineteenth-century models, are incompatible with evolved institutions and evolved ideas of human rights of the late twentieth century. The chances are slim that any of the morally acceptable responses will prove more effective in the twenty-first century in any state with territorial ethnicity, let alone in the new sovereign 'nation-states' that emerged from communist rule. Must we wait for the outbreak of new conflicts, or regional wars, to validate this assessment of the future effect of morally acceptable measures? Does not the war in Bosnia-Herzegovina provide sufficient evidence?

The insistence of foreign governments and international organisations on respect for human rights and protection of 'minorities' will not likely be effective for two principal reasons. First, governments will continue to insist on respecting the principle of 'non-intervention' in the internal affairs of a sovereign state. Second, political entrepreneurs and their mobilised followers will not likely be satisfied with merely gaining the right to vote. They will probably demand self-rule either in the form of autonomy or independent statehood.

There is no intention here to suggest that any of the morally acceptable responses used in the past be abandoned. Just the opposite. The work of various international organisations must be encouraged and supported. Such measures as safeguarding human rights, honouring and protecting minority rights, respecting ethnic and cultural differences and the like, are of indisputable value and should be insisted on. What we do wish to emphasise is that there is no historical evidence that protection of minorities, guarantee of human rights alongside democratisation and economic reforms alone shall prove more effective in the future than they were in the past.

Recent history, since 1985, provides contrary evidence. Even if a cause and effect relationship cannot be established, it is clear that the freeing of the satellite-states from the Soviet Union, the break-up of the Soviet Union itself, the politically expedient recognition of the new states emerging from the former Yugoslavia, and the *introduction of processes of democratisation and concern about human rights* – all preceded the eruption of ethnic conflicts in that part of the world.

What may then be an alternative way toward the reduction of ethnic conflict?

Presenting a different policy aimed at prevention, reduction and ending conflict, especially the one based on the cross-disciplinary approach presented in the previous chapter, requires considerable courage. As our discussion here may have demonstrated, our views counter long-held and deeply felt views. We have gathered the needed courage, for the continuing intensity of ethnic conflicts seems to justify the exploration of every morally acceptable avenue that might lead to their resolution. The threats of ethnic conflicts are prompting new strategic considerations, rearmament, and remilitarisation. These already turn the world away from the peaceful world that just a few years ago many hoped for and expected to materialise rapidly. In addition, economic hardship in new and old states induces the migration of tens of thousands westward – and northward – in search of economic survival and well-being. The new forms of ethnic diversity produced by immigrants in the 'host' countries prompt the activation of right-wing ideologies which favour the above mentioned morally unacceptable measures.

At the base of our 'practical recommendations' is that the various past attempts to 'fit' human beings to artificial 'nation-states' should not continue today, let alone in the twenty-first century.

We are not alone in holding such views. Walker Connor has noted:

> A number of scholars ... voiced strong optimism that ethnonationalism
> can be managed or accommodated within existing political structures.
> A tracing of the history of ethnonationalism and a global survey of its
> current manifestations does not permit this author to share in this
> optimism.[2]

Anthony Smith warned long before the outbreak of ethnic violence
in Yugoslavia:

> ... we must radically change our focus and entrenched positions, if in
> the long term we are to move towards a saner and less brutal world. To
> begin with, the 'international community' must move away from a
> wholly statist analysis to one which is more communally oriented. It
> must break the arid and blind vision of a world of bureaucratic states,
> to which all other potentially political entities must conform or perish.
> This means, for example, that it is no good forcing statist solutions
> onto communally divided areas like Ulster, Cyprus or Lebanon.[3]

Nor onto Bosnia-Herzegovina, one might add. Smith continues:

> ... in the last analysis, [it is] individuals and families whose rights the
> international community ought ultimately to protect,[4]

not the rights of states.

A prominent student of the region, Robert F. Miller, has put it
correctly:

> The principal lesson of the purgatory of B-H, as it is of the fate of the
> first and second Yugoslavia and of Czechoslovakia, is that there are
> limits to the possibilities of synthetic nation-building in multi-ethnic
> regions. The demands for self-determination by insistent minorities
> must evidently somehow be accommodated, however inconvenient
> that may seem to be to geopolitical architects in the 'new world
> order'.[5]

Gidon Gottlieb, noting that the central element in the Wilsonian principle of self-determination was the division of territories, has proposed:

> The principle of self-determination must be supplemented by a new scheme that is less territorial in character and more regional in scope. Such a 'state-plus-nations' approach requires functional spaces and special functional zones across state boundaries, the creation of national home regimes in historical lands, the grant of a recognised status to national communities that have no state of their own ...[6]

An approach that seeks to fit human beings into frameworks, an approach that holds the sovereign state constant and human beings as variables, is not and should not be the acceptable approach. The single framework of the sovereign state is a straitjacket around human beings.

TWO SETS OF NEEDS; TWO SOVEREIGNTIES; TWO FRAMEWORKS

The recommendations we present here are based on the propositions in Chapter 6, namely, that each human being has two sets of needs and that the organism of each compels each to satisfy these needs.

Satisfying psychic or psychological needs is possible in what we called a 'comfortable' socio-political environment, where one can find, for example, a sense of belonging and where the sense of threat is likely to be absent. Such an environment may be found where human beings have similar 'features'. In an ethnically diverse state human beings do not have similar 'features' by definition; such an environment may not be perceived to be 'comfortable'. The centripetal trend mentioned earlier is a trend toward such 'comfortable' environments. Satisfying psychic needs may require an autonomous political entity. The various secessionist movements around the world, including the Bosnian, Muslim, Croat and Serb desires for autonomy are parts of this trend. Most of such attempts are made by territorial ethnic groups and our reference here is only to them.

Now, democracy is *intended* to provide the 'comfortable' socio-political environment, where a diversity of human beings, having different 'features' may elect their own representatives, and find

compromise solutions to problems. It is envisaged that such democratic regimes would eventually emerge in Bosnia-Herzegovina,
Croatia, Romania, Russia and elsewhere. If so, there is no good
reason for Serbs, Hungarians and Chechnyans respectively to secede
or otherwise strive for autonomy. But at the core of democracy is not
reason but will. The right to self-determination is a right to self-rule,
it is a right not to be submitted to rule by a perceived 'other'. Self-
determination is a democratic right. Demanding and providing
self-rule to a group of 'people' who desire it is in clear accordance
with the principle of democracy. Any territorial ethnic group may
claim to be a 'people'. If self-determination is a democratic right,
which it is, then secession is a democratic right too.

A frequently sounded argument is made not against the widely
recognized *right* of secession but against the *impracticality* of secession.
It is that the seceding group, or a break-away group will not be
economically viable.

That this argument is without foundation can easily be shown.
Simply, there are very few economically viable states around the
world; or, to put it differently, the independence of large numbers of
economically non-viable states has been recognised over the last
several decades by the international powers. Neither Slovenia,
Croatia, Bosnia-Herzegovina, nor Slovakia, nor for that matter, the
Baltic states or any other republics of the former Soviet Union, went
through tests of their economic viability. Although a few among
those listed may have passed such a test, economic viability has never
been a criterion for recognition. Rightly so.

Satisfaction of physical needs requires *tangibles*: food, shelter,
health-care, and so on. Food, materials for one's home and clothing –
for one's physical well-being – need not come from a 'comfortable'
socio-political environment; the X-ray machine, the medical doctor,
medications may come from any part of the world. The centrifugal
trend mentioned earlier is a trend toward as wide a framework as
possible, in order to find in the widest economic framework the
tangibles needed for satisfying physical needs.

Now, private enterprise is intended to create an economic environment in which more 'tangibles' would be available. It is possible that
such private enterprise would eventually arrive to such a condition in
every existing state. But physical needs are for 'tangibles', not for

means. In any case, although the economic wealth in a given state, the availability of 'tangibles', may induce an ethnic group not to secede, it is unlikely to induce them to give up their drive to satisfy their psychic needs and not to demand autonomy. This may describe the outcome of repeated referenda in Quebec.

The direction of the centrifugal trend toward the satisfaction of psychic needs is opposite to the direction of the centripetal trend toward the satisfaction of physical needs. The satisfaction of the two sets of needs requires two different organisational arrangements. Here we arrive to the notion of *splitting political sovereignties*.

Sovereignty may briefly, and colloquially, be said to mean superior authority and power; a sovereign is an ultimate decision-maker. However, a distinction may be made between socio-political sovereignty and economic sovereignty. Socio-political sovereignty may be seen as authority and power over interaction among human beings, and pertaining to psychic needs. Economic sovereignty, on the other hand, may be seen as authority and power over tangibles. It supervises interaction that brings about the availability of tangibles for the satisfaction of physical needs.

The state encompasses, in principle, both types of sovereignties: socio-political and economic. Institutions in the state have overall power and authority in matters relating to interaction among its inhabitants, as well as in matters relating, directly or indirectly, to tangibles: export, import, taxes, currency, etc. In federal systems the various institutions are decentralised; in a unitary state they tend to be centralised. In both, boundaries of the state enclose both sovereignties.

Separating the two sovereignties is not only theoretically possible, as we have done above, but it is also possible in practice *if a connection between the two kinds of sovereignties is established*. Socio-political sovereignty may be vested in one type of entity and economic sovereignty in another. The *small* socio-political entities *must be* components of a *wide* economic entity.

Such an arrangement exists, to a degree, in many federal systems, including in the United States. In the United States communities have sovereignty over their educational systems, police, and so on. Each of the 50 states has limited sovereignties in juridical matters for example.

A similar arrangement might have been the result of negotiations that took place prior to the recognition of independence of the break-away republics of Yugoslavia. In February 1992 in Lisbon, the three Bosnian leaders endorsed a proposal that Bosnia be a confederation divided into three ethnic regions. A similar arrangement might have been achieved by the subsequent Vance–Owen and Owen–Stoltenberg proposals of cantonisation, or tripartite division of Bosnia-Herzegovina. These arrangements failed to materialise. The Muslim-dominated Bosnian government wished the recognised Bosnia-Herzegovina to be a unitary state.

The European Union has been variably viewed as cooperation, or a loose federation, or confederation, among independent sovereign states, as an attempt to create a European superstate, or one that is emerging to become a supranational state. However, it may also be viewed as on its way to becoming a wide economic framework composed, eventually, not of sovereign states as they now exist, including both sovereignties, or not only of sovereign states, but also of autonomous entities such as the Welsh and the Basques, which would only have socio-political sovereignties.

One may detect various phases in the evolution of the European Union. The physical and economic devastation of the World War II was overcome, in part, through the generous Marshall Plan to *independent states*, which *reduced* the effect of the centrifugal trend. But the loss of colonies by some of the original members of the European Community, which meant loss of resources and markets, *enhanced* the centrifugal trend and brought about a widening of the economic framework in western Europe. The numerous 'ethnic conflicts' in the 1960s and 1970s – of the Basques, Bretons, and others – may be seen as the centripetal trend.

The European Union is still far from being what is here argued it will eventually become – a wide, mostly economic, framework in which a large number of autonomous socio-political entities are members. Maybe another decade or more is needed to recognise – in retrospect – that process of becoming.

Most, if not all, governments of Central European states – and a majority, or plurality, of their respective populations – appear to be in favour of joining the European Union. Slovenes and Slovaks, for example, do wish such a membership. They probably have no intention of losing their recently gained *national* independence, and probably would not apply if they thought they might. Nevertheless, they both wish to be members in a wide economic framework, which it is proposed here the European Union is, because of prospective *economic* benefits they would gain through such membership. In other words, membership in the European Union is not membership in a superstate in which both political and economic sovereignties are vested. It may simply mean membership in two separate frameworks. Slovenes and Slovaks, for example, could satisfy their psychic needs within Slovenia and Slovakia respectively, and gain a greater chance of satisfying their physical needs as members within the wider framework of the European Union. The membership of these two states in the European Union would also likely reduce the prospects for the activation of ethnic identities, which is prompted by unsatisfied psychological needs. We hypothesise that the 600,000 strong Hungarian minority in Slovakia would be more likely to gain and be granted autonomy, possibly as a precondition for membership in the European Union, than if Slovakia were to remain an independent sovereign state without membership in a wider economic framework.

It may be that membership in the European Union cannot be brought about soon enough to prevent prospects both for the eruption of ethnic conflicts in Central European states and economic hardship for their populations. Their policy makers might possibly opt to form regional framework(s) either alongside the European Union, or perhaps in cooperation with it.

Creation of regional frameworks is not a new idea. There have already been various regional arrangements among Central European states before and after the collapse of communist regimes. Among attempts at regional cooperation one might mention are the Adria-Alpine Group, the Pentagonale, the Visegrad Triangle, and the Tisza-Carpathian group.[7]

The 'Adria-Alpine Group' was formed among states in the Adriatic/ Alpine region in 1978 – long before the end of the Cold War – in order to provide a forum for discussion of largely non-political issues. Members were neutral Austria, Warsaw Pact member Hungary, non-aligned Yugoslavia, and NATO/EC member Italy. Among the concerns, the one relevant here was cultural cooperation.[8] Czechoslovakia applied for membership and was accepted in 1990, and the Group was officially renamed 'Pentagonale' at the Venice summit held 31 July–1 August 1990. Poland's application was accepted and ratified by August 1991 and the Group has become a 'Hexagonale'.

The 'Visegrad Triangle' was organised in February 1991 to include Czechoslovakia, Hungary and Poland. The stated aim of the members was to find broader ties with the European Community. In the summit meeting in Visegrad in February 1991, four goals were posited in a Declaration:

1. restoration in full of each state's independence, democracy and freedom;
2. dismantling of the economic and spiritual structures of the totalitarian system;
3. building of parliamentary democracy and a modern constitutional state, and respect for human rights and fundamental freedoms;
4. total integration into the European political, economic, security and legislative order.[9]

These regional organisations were envisaged as means to attain membership in a free 'Europe' in general and in the European Community/Union in particular. The new regional organisations we propose here may also be considered vehicles for attaining membership in an enlarged European Union.

POLICY RECOMMENDATIONS FOR CENTRAL EUROPEAN STATES

We propose for policy consideration two different kinds of institutions, a *Central European Assembly of Nations* and a *Central European Assembly for Economic Development Coordination*.

A Central European Assembly of Nations could be a representative body of those 'minorities' in Central European states who chose to send elected representatives to it. In order to ensure that only those who activate a separate ethnic/national identity be members, the number of elected representatives from each geographic area would be proportional to the size of the voting population. The purpose of this Assembly would be to hasten the solution of 'minority problems' by serving as an additional channel of communication between 'minorities' and their respective governments. The Assembly would emprovide a forum for discussion of common problems, and for the formulation, publication and submission of recommendations to respective governments and to the international community.

The Central European Assembly for Economic Development Coordination in turn might be composed of representatives of member governments, as well as of various economic sectors in the Central European states and, possibly, of the Central European Assembly of Nations. The purpose of this Assembly is indicated by its name and would be further defined in its constitution.

The Assembly of Nations is intended to cater to psychological needs, 'freedom' and self-rule; the Assembly for Economic Development Coordination is intended to cater to physical needs and serve the human aspiration for 'economic well-being'. The Assembly of Nations would, in the long run, facilitate the consolidation of small self-ruling frameworks; the Assembly for Economic Development Coordination would, in the long run, facilitate the trend toward a wide economic framework.

A Central European Assembly of Nations might reduce the likelihood of ethnic conflicts. They obtain a new forum to air their grievances; and the Central European Assembly for Economic Development Coordination may enhance economic development through cooperative regional projects. Both regional institutions we propose here for consideration are intended to be preparations for and enhance the chances of membership in the European Union.

It does not seem appropriate at this stage to go into specifics as to the name and number of geographic regions and economic sectors that could participate in the two institutions, nor as to the names of Central European states from which representation could be drawn. Suffice it to say that these new institutional arrangements are aimed at better catering to the satisfaction of both sets of needs and thus as instrumental means toward the reduction of the chances for ethnic conflict. At this stage, the proposition could be a topic for discussions among scholars and researchers, representatives of prospective participating states, and representatives of groups who might be participants in the two Assemblies. The 'ethnic mosaic' in Central Europe as examined in Part I may be helpful in suggesting possibilities of regional representation.

CONCLUDING REMARKS

However logical this recommendation may be, politics and not logic rules in the real world. Governments of old and new states in Central Europe will resist it. They will continue to favour *national* consolidation of each sovereign state. They will also promise to safeguard human rights and even extend 'minority rights'. But only as much and as long as these rights do not impinge on the state's sovereignty. To remedy difficult economic conditions within those states, governments will continue to try to expand and strengthen their economic ties, especially trade, and to participate in inter-state economic relations: but only if these ties and relations do not impinge on their economic sovereignty. Governments would oppose the centrifugal and centripetal forces leading toward the formation of two separate frameworks.

That is unfortunate. The emerging dangers to world peace and stability in that part of the world should oblige policy makers not to react to unconventional proposals as if they were mere scholarly exercises. Policy makers should feel obliged to devote time and energy to serious discussion of proposed solutions, including their possible implementation. The democratic earthquake at the end of the Cold War has not produced a peaceful world order. It has merely produced momentum for change.

The new era of change poses new challenges. It may be that the theoretical underpinnings of our policy recommendations will be found faulty. If so, then social scientists, on their part, should come forth with other ideas, overlooked perspectives, and with their own innovative propositions. The emerging dangers to world peace and stability should oblige scholars to break out of conventional scholarly parameters and venture into hitherto unexplored spheres. There is no longer need to consolidate the modern democratic nation-state framework and the old international state system *vis-à-vis* the Soviet Empire. Consequently, it might be *safer* today to recognise as misconceptions both the widely supported theories on the origins and evolution of the state, and the assumed compatibility between national self-determination and the nation-state.

We are ready to enter the competition with other policy proposals coming from social scientists with the following summary of our recommendations.

First, do not be concerned about *economically viable* states but with economically viable *human beings*. In order to reduce conflict – of all types – relevant *physical needs* of human beings must be secured. Most states – especially many of those that broke away from Yugoslavia and the Soviet Union – do not have sufficient amounts and types of human and material resources for satisfying the physical needs of human beings. That may require, in most cases, not merely privatisation, foreign aid and investments; but also membership in an already existing, or newly created, wide economic framework.

Second, do not be concerned about *democratic* states, but about the relevant *psychic needs* of human beings, which do include 'freedom'. It requires, following Anthony Smith's recommendation cited earlier in this chapter, the consideration of the wishes of members in various communities. Providing autonomy to a territorial group who desires it is in accordance with the principle of democracy. Of course, free elections, an important ingredient of the democratic system, are to follow the granting of autonomy. But, democracy without self-rule in freely chosen autonomous entities is truncated democracy.

Switching our concern from the state to human beings would imply a division between economic and political sovereignties which have been enclosed in artificially created states. Political sovereignties would be vested in small, political entities – in order to better satisfy relevant *psychic* needs; they in turn would be confederated in a wide framework where economic sovereignties would be located – in order to better satisfy relevant *physical* needs. Such a complementary trend of change in two directions has been evolving in Europe since western European states lost their membership in the wide economic framework that many of them formed as imperial states. It is likely to proceed elsewhere in the world as well. It is high time to abandon the ideas and structures of the nineteenth century and, instead, to get used to the new realities emerging at the end of the twentieth.

NOTES

1. We are indebted to William Safran for these suggestions conveyed in personal correspondence.

2. Walker Connor, 'The Politics of Ethnonationalism', *Journal of International Affairs*, 27, 1 (1973) p. 20.
3. A.D. Smith, 'Conflict and Collective Identity: Class, *Ethnie* and Nation', in E.E. Azar and J.W. Burton, eds, *International Conflict Resolution, Theory and Practice* (Boulder Co.: Lynne Rienner Publications, 1986), p. 78.
4. Smith, ibid., p. 80.
5. R.F. Miller, 'The Bosnian Tragedy': Historical Roots and Observations', *National Graduate*, The Australian National University (Winter 1993) p. 13.
6. Gidon Gottlieb, 'Nations Without States', *Foreign Affairs*, 73, 3 (May/June 1994) p. 100.
7. The following information is based on an unpublished paper by Sarah Meiklejohn Terry, 'Central European Cooperation in a Post-Communist World', February 1993.
8. On the Adria-Alpine Group see Jonathan Sunley, 'Alpe-Adria: A Community that Works', *East European Reporter*, 4, 2 (Spring/Summer 1990) pp. 59–61.
9. Quoted in Meiklejohn Terry, op. cit., p. 16.

Index

Illyrian movement, the, 41
independence, xxiv, xxv, xxxii, 24, 112, 113,
138; of Bosnia-Herzegovina, 93, 95, 102,
109; of Croatia, 62, 93, 95, 102; in the
Helsinki Final Act, 71; and self-
determination, 64; of Slovenia, 93, 95
India, xv, xix, xx, xxx
Internal Macedonian Revolutionary
Organisation (IMRO), 59
international: community, 103; Covenants
on Human Rights (1966), 69; ethnic
conflict *see* ethnic conflict;
organisations, 139; protection of
minorities, 64; (state) system, 137, 148
intranational ethnic conflict *see* ethnic
conflict
Italians, 30, 54, 62
Italy, xv, xvi, xix, 28, 32, 37, 43, 50, 53;
member of the Adria-Alpine Group, 145
Izetbegovic, Alija, 93, 94, 104

Janissaries, 6, 24
Jaszi, Oszkar, 47
Jews, xxiv, xxxiv, 114
Joseph II, Emperor, 16, 18
Judah, Tim, 96
Jura problem, xvi

Kann, Robert, 37, 41, 45
Karadjordevic dynasty, 80
Karadzic, Radovan, 94
Karolyi, Mihály, 47
Karpat, Kamal, 22, 26, 27
Kingdom of Serbs, Croats and Slovenes,
becomes Yugoslavia (1929), 8, 80
Kosovo, xxiii, xxv, 29, 77, 81, 82, 87, 95, 101,
105n; Battle of, 6, 80; Kosovo Provincial
Assembly, 105n
Kossuth, Lajos, 34, 35
Krajina region, 7, 8, 42, 90, 92

language families/differences, 4ff., 122
Latvia, xxiv, xxxi
Latvians, in the USSR, xxiv
Lawson, Stephanie, 129
League of Nations, 53, 54, 55, 57, 70;
Covenant of the, 50, 54
Lenin, V.I., 48
liberal democracy *see* democracy
linguistic groups, xv
Lisbon: agreement, 94; meeting of
February 1992, 93
Lithuania, xxi, xxxi; Lithuanian
parliament, xxxi
Lithuanians, xxiv
Lloyd George, David, 49
Lusatians, 5, 6, 14, 19n,

Macedonia, xxiii, 10, 59, 81, 88
Macedonian identity, 10
Macedonians, xxiii, 4–6, 10, 47

Magyarisation (of minorities), 8, 14, 38, 42
Magyar nationalism, 36; *see also* Hungary
Magyars *see* Hungarians
Mahmud II, 24
majority, xix, xx, 112; Croatian, xxiii; rule,
xx, 110; status, xviii
March Laws of 1848, 34
Maria Theresa, 16
Marx, Karl, xiv, 130
Marxism, 130
Marxist ideology, xiv, 49
Masaryk, Jan, 55
Masaryk, Thomas, 43, 46, 65
Matthias, King, 12
Mazzini, Joseph, 33
Mejid, Abdul, 24
memories of past atrocities, 100, 102
Metternich, 32, 33, 34
Miller, Robert, 87
millet (system), 20–7, 29
Milosevic, Slobodan, 82, 91, 92
minority(ies), xvii, xix, xx, 45, 137, 146;
based government, xix; Bosnian-Serb,
113; in decolonisation, 69; during the
Cold War, 71; in the Helsinki Final Act,
72; in Hungary, 35, 38, 40; and the
League of Nations, 70; minority
problems, 48, 58, 60, 73, 146; minority
rights, 57, 70, 72, 74, 138, 139, 148;
policies towards, 132; protection of, 137;
in the republics of Yugoslavia, 85, 86;
Serbian, 90; treatment of, 41; and the
UN Charter, 63; in Western European
states, 136; after World War I, 135
Minority Protection System, 70
Minority Treaties, 57, 70
missionaries (in the Ottoman Empire), 22
modernisation, xv, 24, 25, 27, 28, 36, 43, 49
Mohacs, defeat of the Hungarians by
Ottomans at, 17
Moldava, 74
Moldavia, xxiii
Moldavians, xxiii
Montenegrins, 5, 6, 11, 26
Montenegro, 11, 81, 88, 95, 97
Moravia, 11, 12, 58
Moravian Empire, 12, 13
Moravians, 13, 16, 30, 39
Moscow, xxiii, xxiv, 84
Munich appeasement/Pact (1938), 58, 65
Muslims *see* Bosnians; Bosnian Muslims
Mussolini, 59

Nagorno-Karabagh *see* Azerbidjan
Napoleonic Wars, 31, 32
nation, 28, 112ff.; nation-building, xxxi,
xxxiii
national: aspirations of Bosnian Serbs and
Croats, xxxii; awakening, 24;
consciousness, 23; entities, 86;
identity(ies), xxxi, 23, 33, 124;